Mastering Reading

Learning About Office Work Book 3

Jean Bernard-Johnston
Linda S. Lee
Alice Lyons-Quinn

Delmar Occupational Learning System®

NOTICE TO THE READER

Publisher does not warrant or guarantee any of the products described herein or perform any independent analysis in connection with any of the product information contained herein. Publisher does not assume, and expressly disclaims, any obligation to obtain and include information other than that provided to it by the manufacturer.

The reader is expressly warned to consider and adopt all safety precautions that might be indicated by the activities described herein and to avoid all potential hazards. By following the instructions contained herein, the reader willingly assumes all risks in connection with such instructions.

The publisher makes no representations or warranties of any kind, including but not limited to, the warranties of fitness for particular purpose or merchantability, nor are any such representations implied with respect to such material. The publisher shall not be liable for any special, consequential or exemplary damages resulting, in whole or in part, from the readers' use, or reliance upon, this material.

Photos courtesy of Joseph Arn, Paul Meyers, Jeff Greenberg, Knight-Ridder and Ford Motor Company

Delmar staff:
Executive Editor: David C. Gordon
Project Editor: Judith Boyd Nelson
Production Coordinator: Teresa Luterbach
Art Supervisor: John Lent
Design Supervisor: Susan C. Mathews

For information, address Delmar Publishers, Inc.
2 Computer Drive, West, Box 15-015,
Albany, NY 12212-9985

COPYRIGHT © 1991
BY DELMAR PUBLISHERS INC.

All right reserved. No part of this work covered by the copyright hereon may be reproduced or used in any form or by any means—graphic, electronic, or mechanical, including photocopying, recording, taping, or information storage and retrieval systems—without written permission of the publisher.

Printed in the United States of America
Published simultaneously in Canada
by Nelson Canada
A Division of The Thomson Corporation

10 9 8 7 6 5 4 3 2 1

ISBN 0-8273-4540-2

CONTENTS

UNIT	1	On Your Own: Inside a Small Office	1
UNIT	2	Teamwork: Inside a Large Office	7
UNIT	3	Following Through	13
UNIT	4	May I Help You?	19
UNIT	5	One Moment, Please	25
UNIT	6	Check the Time	31
UNIT	7	The A, B, Cs of Filing	37
UNIT	8	What's the Password?	43
UNIT	9	Mail It	49
UNIT	10	Preparing Outgoing Mail	55
UNIT	11	From Words to Letters	63
UNIT	12	It's All in the Details	69
UNIT	13	Getting the Message	75
UNIT	14	The Electronic Office	81
UNIT	15	In Good Time	87
UNIT	16	Look It Up	93
UNIT	17	Getting the Facts	101
UNIT	18	Stressing the Limits	107
UNIT	19	What Makes a Good Employee?	113
UNIT	20	Starting Out Right	119
		Answer Keys	125
		Glossary	169

TO THE LEARNER

Welcome to *Mastering Reading: Learning About Office Work, Book 3*. All the books in the Office Work series are written with you, the adult learner, in mind. As you know, being able to read well is very important in the world of today. With good reading skills, you have a much better chance of getting the kind of job you want. Good reading skills can also help you to move ahead in the job you already have.

You will be able to improve your reading skills as you go through this book, and at the same time, you will learn something about Office Work.

Book 3 is made up of 20 lessons. You can look at the **Table of Contents** to see what they are about. Each lesson begins with some questions on the first page. There are no right or wrong answers to these questions. Examples of questions are, "What kinds of skills do you think a receptionist should have?" and "How often do you make telephone calls to people outside of your state?" These questions let you look at and think about some things that you have already learned. That way, the lesson will make more sense to you. Some of you reading this book will be in a class with other students. If so, your instructor will probably have you talk about these questions together as a class. If you are working alone with a tutor, you can discuss your ideas with the tutor.

Each lesson has two pages of reading. Most of these readings are about different jobs in an office. As you read, you will notice that some words are in **boldface**. These bold-faced words are explained in the **Glossary** in the back of the book. The Glossary tells you what each bold-faced word means. After you read the meaning, you will find one or two sentences using that word.

After each reading, you will find two to three pages of exercises. These exercises ask questions that are based on the reading or on your own experience in life. There are two kinds of exercises in each lesson:

- a Review exercise
- two or more Practice exercises

Answers for all the Review and Practice exercises are in the back of the book in the **Answer Key** located just before the Glossary. The Answer Key lets you check your answers and correct them if you need to.

The Review questions have three possible answers to choose from. To find the right answers, you may want to go back and do the reading again. You will probably discuss your answers with people in your class and with your teacher. The first Review question in each lesson is answered for you.

There are many different kinds of Practice exercises. Some exercise questions have just one right answer. Others have more than one correct answer. These types of Practice exercises will have the words: "More than one answer is possible. Check with your instructor or tutor." With these exercises, each learner might have a different answer. For example, the question "What is your opinion?" would have many answers. Each answer would be correct for the person giving it.

When you have read *Mastering Reading: Learning About Office Work, Book 3*, you may wish to continue with *Mastering Reading: Learning About Office Work, Book 4*. This book will give you more useful information about Office Work and what it is like to work in an office.

Some adult learners will use these books to get information about careers in Office Work. Others may read the books to improve their reading skills. Whatever reason you have, we hope that you are able to enjoy this book and to learn from it. Good Luck!

UNIT 1

On Your Own: Inside a Small Office

This unit is about:

- how a small office operates
- duties of an office worker

Think About

Would you rather work in a small office or a large office? Why?
What types of work do you think an office worker does?

On Your Own: Inside a Small Office

"I enjoy my work," explains Tony Rivera, "because every day is different. I'm pretty much on my own in the office, and there are a lot of different things to do. I'm almost never bored."

Tony works for Ben's Body Shop, a small business that employs ten auto body technicians. The technicians repair body damage on cars and trucks. The customers pay for the work, and the employees receive a salary.

Ben, the owner, is also the **manager** of the business. Until a few years ago, Ben did all of the office work himself. He had to work very long hours—60 to 70 hours a week. When his business started to make more money, he decided to hire a full-time office worker. He interviewed several applicants and chose Tony. Although all of the applicants had good office skills, Ben felt that Tony was the best person for the job.

Ben needed someone with a pleasant personality. The person had to get along well with the customers and the other employees. He also needed someone who could work **independently**, without much supervision. In other words, he needed someone who could keep the office running smoothly.

Tony's office is small. There are only two desks, a closet for supplies, and two filing cabinets. Most of the time, Tony works in the office alone. On a typical day, Tony is responsible for:

- dealing with customers
- answering the phone and making appointments
- making up bills and receiving payments
- keeping a record of money received and paid out
- ordering parts and supplies
- opening and sorting mail
- filing important papers and letters

An **accountant** comes in for a few days each month. She helps Tony keep track of the money coming in and going out of the office. The accountant also helps make out the **payroll** so that all of the employees can get paid.

Tony believes that the most important part of his job is **customer relations**. "You can lose a customer just by forgetting to smile," he says. Tony makes a point of being friendly, even when giving information over the telephone. "The way you say something is just as important as what you say," he adds.

What other advice would Tony give someone looking for a job in a small office?

- Be a self-starter. Don't wait around for someone to tell you what to do. Try to develop your own daily routines.

- Stay organized. File papers away and clear your desk at the end of each day. Always know where things are.

- Be **flexible.** Always be willing to stop what you are doing to help a customer.

It takes a special kind of person to work in a small office. These employees may have to do a variety of jobs. They may have to work without a lot of supervision. But for a person like Tony, it is the right kind of job.

REVIEW

Choose the best answer. Circle it. Go back to the reading to check your answers. The first one is done for you.

1. Why does Tony enjoy his job?
    a. He likes working with a large group of people.
    (b.) He gets to do different things.
    c. He is told exactly what to do each day.
    d. He gets to do the same thing all day.

2. Which of the following is not one of Tony's responsibilities?
    a. dealing with customers
    b. opening and sorting mail
    c. interviewing applicants
    d. filing important papers and letters

3. Why do you think a pleasant personality is important in Tony's job?
    a. Because he always works alone.
    b. Because he has to deal with customers.
    c. Because he does the payroll.
    d. Because he works independently.

4. An accountant is a person who _____.
    a. keeps track of money
    b. orders parts and supplies
    c. repairs damage on cars
    d. opens and sorts mail

5. According to Tony, the way you say something is just as important as what you say. Based on this, which statement do you think Tony would make to a customer?
    a. What do you want?
    b. I can't talk to you now. Call back later.
    c. Do you want help?
    d. How can I help you?

6. A person who is a self-starter might say, _____.
    a. "I have a little free time. I think I'll check the files."
    b. "I wish the boss would tell me what to do next."
    c. "I don't have anything to do. I guess I'll just sit here."
    d. "When the boss returns, I'll ask him what to do next."

PRACTICE

A. Who are they? Use the job descriptions to identify the people at Ben's Body Shop. Choose from the list below and look back at the reading if necessary. Write the names of the jobs on the right side of the box. The first one is done for you.

>   accountant   auto body technician
>   manager   office worker   owner

Job Description	Job Title
Repairs body damage on cars and trucks.	auto body technician
Manages the whole business, makes all important decisions. Hires and fires employees.	
Deals with customers, keeps records, answers telephones, opens mail, files papers, keeps the office running smoothly.	
Checks records of money received and paid out, does the payroll.	
Owns the business. May also take part in business decisions.	

B. Predict the questions. Imagine that you are going to an interview for a job in a small office. Read the job description, then write four questions that the interviewer might ask. An example is provided for you.

> **Job Description**
> Take charge of organizing and running a small office. Successful applicant will have excellent office skills, pleasant personality, and ability to work independently. Computer experience helpful. Applicant should be flexible and willing to learn.

Interview questions:

1. _Do you have any experience working in a small office?_
2. _____
3. _____
4. _____
5. _____

C. What are your strengths? On the chart below, list your skills and personal qualities. Give more details for personal qualities in the spaces on the right. An example is provided for you.

Skills	Excellent	Fair	Poor
Filing		√	

Personal Qualities	Details
Friendly	I enjoy meeting people.

UNIT 2

Teamwork: Inside a Large Office

This unit is about:

- how a large office is organized
- the duties of an office worker in a large office

Think About

Think of some large companies in you area. What types of jobs are there in these companies?
Would you like to work in a large office? Why?

Teamwork: Inside a Large Office

"I like working in a large office because you can always get help when you need it," says Vera Bromley. Vera has been working for the Reliance Insurance Company for almost five years.

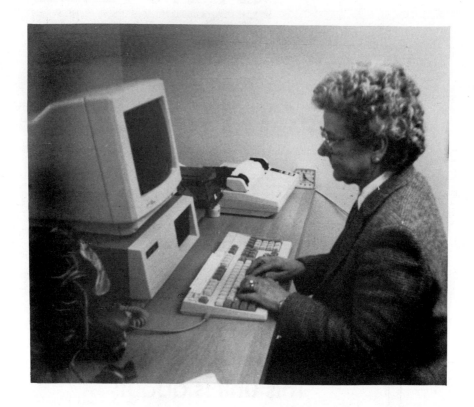

"There are other **benefits** too," Vera adds. "Besides a good health care program, the company offers training programs for employees who want to improve their skills. There's always a chance to get ahead if you really want to."

Vera's first job with the company was in the **records management** department. This department takes care of the important papers in the company. As a **file clerk**, Vera spent most of her time working on customer files. When the office manager offered her the chance to learn **word processing**, she agreed immediately. After completing the training program, Vera joined the word processing center as a **trainee.** After six months, she became a word processing operator. Now she makes $4000 a year more than she did as a file clerk.

Large companies are divided into **departments**. Each department has its own **support staff**, or group of office workers. In Vera's department, there are 26 office workers, 3 supervisors, and the office manager. The office manager is in charge of the support staff. She reports directly to the head of the department. The chart below shows how the support staff is organized.

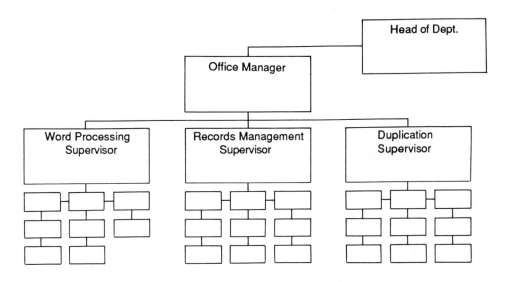

The word processing center, where Vera works, provides services for the whole department. Her supervisor receives job requests and schedules the work.

The people in records management take care of all the documents in the department. The clerks who work there must learn the company's filing system. They must know how to file and to retrieve, or get, information from files.

When Vera needs copies of documents, letters, or reports, she sends a request to the duplication section. There, the machine operators make the copies.

What does it take to succeed in a large office? "Teamwork!" smiles Vera. "You have to be willing to pull together, especially when there is a lot of work to do."

REVIEW

Choose the best answer. Circle it. Go back to the reading to check your answers. The first one is done for you.

1. Vera's first job at the company was in _____.
    a. management
    (b.) records management
    c. word processing
    d. duplication

2. Which of these might be another one of the benefits of working at the Reliance Insurance Company?
    a. no pay when you are sick
    b. little chance for advancement
    c. paid vacation
    d. low salaries

3. A trainee is an employee who ____.
    a. is learning a new job
    b. supervises other employees
    c. assists with schedules and reports
    d. provides services for the whole department

4. The three supervisors of the office support staff report to _____.
    a. Vera
    b. the office manager
    c. the file clerks
    d. the head of the department

5. Who probably has the highest salary?
    a. a file clerk
    b. a word processing supervisor
    c. a word processing trainee
    d. a machine operator

6. Another title for this unit might be _____.
    a. How to Get a Job in Records Management
    b. The Word Processing Center
    c. How a Large Office Is Organized
    d. The Differences in Offices

PRACTICE

A   Who are they? Read the job descriptions and identify the members of the office support staff. Look back at the reading if necessary. Write the names of the jobs on the right side of the box. An example is provided for you.

file clerk   machine operator   office manager
word processing operator   word processing supervisor

Job Description	Job Title
Files and retrieves documents.	File clerk
Operates duplicating machines. Makes copies of documents, letters, and reports.	
Operates word processing equipment. Produces letters, documents, and reports.	
Supervises workers in the word processing center. Receives job requests and schedules work.	
Is in charge of supervisors and office workers. Reports directly to the department head.	

B.   What is the difference? Vera described some of the good things about working in a large office. Can you think of some other good things about working in a large office? List these on the left side of the chart below. Then list some of the good things about working in a small office on the right side of the chart. An example of each is provided.

Working in a Large Office	Working in a Small Office
You can get help easily.	You get to do different things.

11

C. Who's in charge here? Read the paragraph below. Then fill in the chart of Vera's office with the names of the people in each position. The first one is done for you.

Marie Datcher is head of the customer claims department. Over 80 employees work in this department. The office support staff is a very important part of the department. The office manager, Ms. Sheila Kaminsky, is in charge of a staff of 29. The three supervisors report directly to her. Mr. Ted Carter, Vera's supervisor, is in charge of word processing. The records management supervisor is Ms. Tanh Nguyen. The supervisor of the duplicating center, Renaldo Garcia, worked his way up from an entry-level position. Together, the whole office staff works as a team to provide important services to the department.

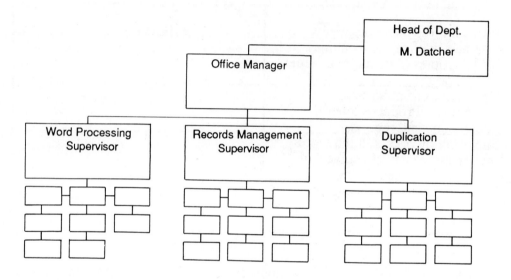

UNIT 3

Following Through

This unit is about:

- working in an insurance company
- how departments in a large company work together

Think About

Think of three ways that workers in large offices communicate with each other.
What kinds of departments do you think an insurance company has?

Following Through

When Tony walked into the Quick Stop Clinic with a bad cold, this was the first question the receptionist asked: "Do you have health insurance?"

Tony answered that he was on a company insurance plan. He showed the receptionist his insurance card. She wrote down some information from the card before she let Tony see the doctor. Tony smiled. He was glad he had insurance.

Tony's employer, Ben's Body Shop, has a health insurance plan for all employees. When an employee gets sick or has an accident, all or part of the medical costs are **covered** by the Reliance Insurance Company. Every month, Ben's Body Shop pays the insurance company an amount of money to keep the plan.

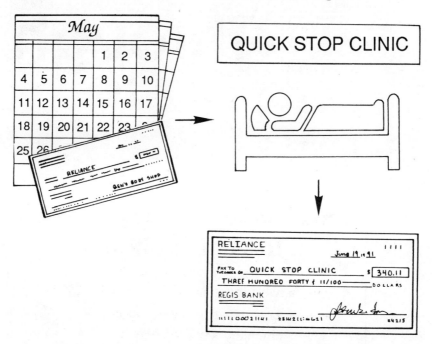

When Tony felt better, he filled out an insurance **claim** for the cost of his medical care. He sent the claim to the Reliance Insurance Company. Here is what happened to the claim:

1. The mailroom at the insurance company received Tony's claim. They sent it to the claims department through the **interoffice** mail.

2. Sylvia DuBois, a **claims representative**, received Tony's claim. She had to decide how much the company would pay on Tony's insurance claim. Sylvia called records management to ask for Tony's file. She studied the file and decided that the company would pay the whole bill.

3   Sylvia asked the word processing center to prepare a letter for Tony. A word processor typed the letter and sent it back to Sylvia for her signature.

4   Sylvia asked the duplication department to make copies of the claim and the letter. Then she **forwarded** a copy of the claim to the accounting department. This department would make out a check and send it to the Quick Stop Clinic.

5   Sylvia put Tony's letter in the outgoing mail. She put a copy of the claim and the letter in Tony's file and returned it to records management.

The mailroom, the claims department, and the accounting department at Reliance worked together to **process** Tony's claim in just a few days. When Tony got the good news, he told his employer about it.

"Good," said Ben. "Some of the other companies are less expensive, but this one has the best service. I guess we'll stick with Reliance."

REVIEW

Choose the best answer. Circle it. Go back to the reading to check your answers. The first one is done for you.

1. Who pays for Tony's health insurance?
    a. Tony
    (b.) his employer
    c. Vera
    d. Reliance

2. The receptionist wanted to be certain that _____.
    a. Tony had been there before
    b. Tony had a job
    c. Tony was really sick
    d. someone would pay the bill

3. How much of Tony's bill was paid by Reliance Insurance Company?
    a. a large amount of it
    b. all of it
    c. part of it
    d. half of it

4. What is Sylvia DuBois's job?
    a. She makes decisions about insurance claims.
    b. She supervises the mailroom.
    c. She makes copies of documents.
    d. She is a word processor.

5. When Tony's employer heard the news about the insurance claim, he decided to _____.
    a. change insurance companies
    b. stop paying the insurance bill
    c. keep the same plan
    d. call up the claims department

6. Another title for this unit could be _____.
    a. What Happens to Your Insurance Claim
    b. What Happens When You Have an Accident
    c. Filling Out a Form
    d. Getting Medical Help

PRACTICE

A Put them in order. The sentences below explain how a claim is processed at the Reliance Insurance Company. Put the steps in the correct order by writing the correct number in each space. Look back at the reading if you need help. The first one is done for you.

_____ The claims representative makes a decision.

_____ Tony receives a letter.

__1__ Tony fills out a claim and sends it to the insurance company.

_____ A word processing operator prepares a letter.

_____ Copies of the letter and the claim are made.

_____ The mailroom receives Tony's claim.

_____ A file clerk retrieves Tony's file.

_____ The people in the mailroom send Tony's claim to a claims representative.

B. Where is it done? Read each sentence and decide where each job is done. Choose from the list below. Write the name of the department next to the sentence.

   Mailroom   Claims   Accounting

__Mailroom_____   1. Someone sorts the mail.

_____   2. Someone prepares checks.

_____   3. Payments from customers are received.

_____   4. Word processors write letters to customers.

_____   5. Someone decides on the amount of payment on claims.

17

C. Would you sign this letter? This letter was prepared by a word processor in the claims department, but it has some spelling errors. Find and underline the three errors. Then write the words correctly on the lines below the letter. An example is provided for you.

RELIANCE INSURANCE CO.
"You Can Rely On Us"

January 12, 1991

Mr. Anthony Rivera
Ben's Body <u>Ship</u>
12 Main St.
Carbondale, IL 62901

Dear Mr. Rivera:

I am pleased to infrom you that your claim of 12/15/90 (Ref. # 679213) has been approved. The cost of the care provided by Quick Stop Clinic, Inc. of Carbondale is covered in full by your group health insurunce plan. Payment will be made directally to the provider. If I can be of further assistance, please do not hesitate to contact me.

Sincerely,

Sylvia M. DuBois

Sylvia M. DuBois
Claims Representative

    <u>shop</u>

_____

_____

_____

UNIT 4

May I Help You?

This unit is about:

- the duties of a receptionist
- dealing with problems at the reception desk

Think About

Why is a receptionist's job important?
What kinds of skills do you think a receptionist should have?

May I Help You?

When you visit or call an office, the first person you usually speak to is the receptionist. The word *reception* comes from *receive*, which means to greet or welcome visitors. Thus, the main responsibility of an office receptionist is to greet and assist people who come in or call.

In many offices, people will call before they come in. This is why the receptionist must have excellent telephone skills. She must be able to direct incoming calls to the right person or department. She may also have to **screen** calls, or find out who is calling and why.

When a visitor arrives at the office, the receptionist must find out whom the person wants to see. Visitors who have an appointment will usually give their name and the details of the appointment. If not, it is the receptionist's job to ask, as in the example below.

Receptionist: Good morning, may I help you?
Visitor: I have a ten o'clock appointment with Ms. Ly.
Receptionist: May I have your name, please?
Visitor: Oh, yes, of course. I'm Joe Morgan of Sunflower Cleaning Services.
Receptionist: Thank you, Mr. Morgan. I'll let her know you're here. Please have a seat.

Anna Valdez is an experienced receptionist at a large insurance company. She says that there are times when she is ready to tear her hair out. She may, for example, receive several calls all at once. She may have to put one or more callers on hold while she takes each incoming call in turn. She must know whether her boss is free to receive telephone calls. At the same time, one or more visitors may arrive, each needing help and attention.

"Above all, stay calm," advises Anna, "even if callers or visitors become **impatient**."

Sometimes, too, visitors may be pushy or rude even when the receptionist is polite and helpful. A visitor may simply drop in without an appointment and **demand** to see someone right away. When this happens, the receptionist should follow office instructions.

Then there are times when the telephone is silent, and there are no visitors waiting in the reception area. Many receptionists are expected to perform other **tasks**, such as light typing or filing, during these times. These tasks can be **interrupted** easily whenever the telephone rings or a visitor arrives. Above all, a receptionist's job is to deal with each person in a warm, friendly way, even when things get tough. A good receptionist tries hard to remain pleasant, calm, and polite.

REVIEW

Choose the best answer. Circle it. Go back to the reading to check your answers. The first one is done for you.

1. A receptionist's major responsibilities are to _____.
    a. open mail and make outgoing calls
    b. file important papers and type letters
    (c.) receive visitors and take incoming calls
    d. set up schedules and invite visitors

2. It is most important for a receptionist to have _____.
    a. good typing skills
    b. computer experience
    c. excellent telephone skills
    d. good math skills

3. The conversation in the reading shows how to _____.
    a. stop a visitor from entering an office
    b. screen a call
    c. ask a visitor for information
    d. put a caller on hold

4. What do you think a good receptionist would say if a visitor demanded to see someone immediately?
    a. "She's busy now. You can't see her."
    b. "Please have a seat. I will tell her you are here."
    c. "Why don't you go and find her?"
    d. "You are making me nervous. Sit down."

5. What is the best thing to do when a visitor comes in without an appointment?
    a. Let the visitor walk right in.
    b. Tell the visitor to go away.
    c. Find out what the person wants.
    d. Direct the visitor to the boss.

6. Another title for this unit might be _____.
    a. How to Be Polite
    b. The Receptionist's Job
    c. Working in an Office
    d. Making Appointments

PRACTICE

A Choose the best way to say it. For each pair of sentences, choose the question a receptionist should ask when greeting a visitor or handling an incoming call. Check (√) the more polite question. The first one is done for you.

1. __√__   May I ask who's calling?
   _____   Who are you?

2. _____   What do you want?
   _____   May I help you?

3. _____   He's not in at the moment. May I take a message?
   _____   He's not here. I can't help you.

4. _____   Good morning, Life Associates. Can you hold for a moment?
   _____   Good morning, I'm on another line. You'll have to wait.

5. _____   What are you doing here without an appointment?
   _____   Would you like to make an appointment?

6. _____   What is your telephone number?
   _____   May I have your number, please?

B. Make it polite. Put each of these sentences in a more polite form. Write your sentences on the blank lines. The first one is done for you.

1. Why are you here?

   Do you have an appointment to see someone?

2. Why are you calling?

   _____

3. You can't talk to Ms. Ly now. She's busy.

   _____

C. What would you do? Read the instructions to the receptionist from Bruce Chen, a supervisor at Life Associates. Based on the instructions, explain what you would do in each situation. An example is provided for you.

**From the Desk of:
Bruce Chen**

To: Anna
From: Bruce
Re: Incoming Calls and Visitors

1. Put through any time
   -Mr. Jason Burks (owner)
   -Ms. An Ly
   -Mr. David Berzinski
   -all long distance callers

2. Take a message from
   -Ms. Savan Phun
   -Dr. Kevin Brown
   -Mr. Julio Pena

3. <u>Never</u> allow in
   -visitors without appointments

---

1. You receive a long distance call for Mr. Chen.

   I would put the call through right away.

2. Mr. David Berzinski asks to speak to Mr. Chen.

   _____

3. Dr. Kevin Brown asks to speak to Mr. Chen.

   _____

4. A salesperson drops in without an appointment. He wants to see Mr. Chen.

   _____

5. A salesperson calls from another state.

   _____

UNIT 5

One Moment, Please

This unit is about:

- using an office telephone
- telephone manners

Think About

Have you ever been cut off while you were talking on the telephone? What did you do?
Has anyone ever been rude to you on telephone? What did you do?

One Moment, Please

It is Gerald's first day in the office. It is a small office, but there are still a lot of things to remember. He stares at the telephone. It is different from his telephone at home. This telephone has a red key, or pushbutton, labeled HOLD. It also has five **line keys**. Each line key is for a different telephone number. That means that five people can call at the same time! A different four-digit number is written under each key. These are the last four digits of the telephone number.

Each line key has a red **indicator light.** If someone in the office is using a telephone line, the indicator light goes on and stays on. If an indicator light goes on and off as the telephone rings, a call is coming in on that line.

Soon after 9:00 a.m., the telephone rings. The 2401 indicator light goes on and off. Gerald presses the 2401 key and picks up the **receiver**.

Gerald: Cool Spring Water Company, Gerald Barnes speaking. May I help you?
Caller: You certainly may. I want to know where my water is.
Gerald: May I ask who's calling?
Caller: Yes, this is Yusef Saleh of City Gym.
Gerald: One moment please, I'll transfer you to our customer service representative.

The telephone rings again. Gerald answers it. The caller asks to speak to Ms. Minh, the customer service representative. He looks at the telephone. The indicator light on Ms. Minh's line is lit.

Gerald: I'm sorry, Ms. Minh is on another line. May I take a message?
Caller: Yes, please. This is Judy Hall of Judy's Office Supply. Tell her that I have a question about my bill. Ask her to get back to me as soon as she can.
Gerald: May I have your number, please?
Caller: It's 738-1209.
Gerald: 7-3-8, 1-2-0-9. I'll give her the message right away.
Caller: Thank you, good-bye.

Later that afternoon the phone rings while Gerald is talking to a customer on line 2401.

"I'm sorry, I have another call," he explains to the customer. "Can you hold for just a moment?" Gerald transfers the incoming call to Ms. Minh, then presses 2401 again. He thanks the customer for waiting and continues the conversation.

By the end of the day, Gerald feels better about using the office telephone. He only made one mistake. One time he forgot to press the HOLD button before he pressed another key. This cut the caller off. When she called again, Gerald **apologized** and thanked her for calling back. He was happy that she did not get angry.

REVIEW

Choose the best answer. Circle it. Go back to the reading to check your answers. The first one is done for you.

1. What happens to a line key when the line is in use?
    a. it flashes on and off rapidly
    b. it rings
    c. nothing
    ⓓ. the indicator light goes on and stays on

2. What does a rapidly flashing indicator light mean?
    a. someone is using the line
    b. a caller is on hold
    c. someone is making a long distance call
    d. someone is calling out

3. Judy Hall wanted Ms. Minh to ____ as soon as possible.
    a. return her call
    b. take a message
    c. deliver her water
    d. send her a bill

4. How would you describe Gerald's telephone manners while he was talking to Yusef Saleh?
    a. Gerald was rude.
    b. Gerald was polite and patient.
    c. Gerald did not sound friendly.
    d. Gerald's telephone manners made Yusef angry.

5. How did Gerald cut off one caller?
    a. by hanging up on her
    b. by forgetting to press the HOLD button
    c. by transferring her to Ms. Minh
    d. by talking too long on another line

6. What would be the best thing to say to the caller he cut off?
    a. "I'm sorry...thank you for calling back."
    b. "May I take a message?"
    c. "It wasn't my fault!"
    d. "Please don't tell Ms. Minh."

PRACTICE

A. Choose a word. Choose a word from the list below to complete each sentence. The first one is done for you.

indicator lights   line   on hold   receiver   transferred

1. When Gerald's phone rang, one of the __indicator lights__ flashed on and off.

2. Gerald could not answer the caller's question, so he _____ the call to his supervisor.

3. Gerald put the caller _____ so that he could transfer the call.

4. When the phone rang, Gerald picked up the _____.

5. Gerald was talking on one _____ when another person called.

B. What would you say? Read each of the following situations. Explain what you would say to the caller. Write your ideas on the blank lines. The first one is done for you.

1. The caller wants to speak to Mr. Morgan, but he is not in the office.

   __I'm sorry, he's not in. May I take a message?__

2. You are giving a caller some information. While you are talking, a call comes in on another line.

   _____

   _____

3. You have asked a caller to wait while you take an incoming call. You now take the first caller off hold and start speaking.

   _____

   _____

4. You have cut off a caller by mistake. The same person calls again.

   _____

   _____

C. Take a message. A customer calls and gives you the information below. Use the telephone message form to take a message based on the information. The form is started for you.

"Please tell Mr. Romero that Ms. Jane Miller of Duplex Services called. Yes, that's Duplex, D-U-P-L-E-X Services. It's not really urgent, it's about our appointment tomorrow. Tell him I simply won't be able to make it. I have to go out of town. Ask him to call me before 5:00 so we can schedule another meeting next week. Thanks so much."

```
To    Mr. Romero
Date_____  Time_____
```

While You Were Out

```
M _____
Of _____
Phone No _____
```

Telephoned		Please Call	
Was in to see you		Will call again	

Message

By _____

UNIT 6

Check the Time

This unit is about:

- placing long distance calls
- services of the telephone company

Think About

How often do you make telephone calls to people outside of your state? What do you have to remember to do when you make calls to other parts of the country?

Check the Time

After a few days on the job at Cool Spring Water Company, Gerald had gotten used to the phone system. He felt that he could handle just about anything.

Today Gerald got to work a little before 9 a.m. As soon as he was at his desk, Ms. Minh buzzed him. "Gerald, could you please place a call for me to Mr. Thomas at National Shipping. The number is (601) 439-3426."

Gerald dialed the number and heard the phone ring. It rang and rang but no one answered. "That's strange," Gerald said to himself. He waited a few minutes and tried the number again. The same thing happened. Gerald buzzed Ms. Minh on the intercom. "I'm sorry, Ms. Minh, but no one answers," explained Gerald.

"No one answered?" asked Ms. Minh. "It's a large office. I can't believe that no one is there. Are you sure you dialed the right number?"

"I think so," Gerald answered. "I dialed (601) 439-3426. That's the right number, isn't it?" Then Gerald remembered something. "601 is the area code for Mississippi," Gerald said to Ms. Minh. "Mississippi is in another time zone. That means it is only 8 a.m. in Mississippi. The office isn't open yet."

"Of course," said Ms. Minh. "I forgot about that. I guess we will have to wait an hour and then you can place the call again. Thanks for reminding me, Gerald."

Whenever you make a long distance or **international** call, it is important to be aware of time differences. For a call within the United States, you can check the map in the front of your phone book. It will tell you if the place you are calling is in a different time zone. As the map below shows, there is a time difference of three hours between the East Coast and the West Coast. In other words, when it is 4 p.m. in New York, it is only 1 p.m. in California.

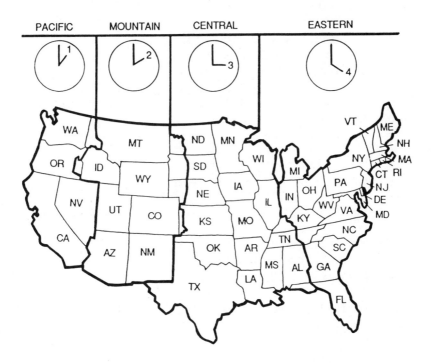

Later in the day, Ms. Minh asked Gerald to arrange a **conference call**. This type of call allows three or more people in different places to talk at the same time. Ms. Minh gave Gerald the names and phone numbers of the people she needed to talk to. To arrange the conference call, Gerald first called each of the **participants** and set up the time for the call. Then he called the operator and gave her the names and phone numbers of the participants. He also gave the exact time he wanted the call to take place.

Telephone service has improved greatly in the past few decades. You can now dial direct to someone in another state or country. You can talk to more than one person at the same time by arranging a conference call. What services do you think we will have in the future?

REVIEW

Choose the best answer. Circle it. Go back to the reading to check your answers. The first one is done for you.

1. What happened when Gerald called National Shipping?
    a. Mr. Thomas was busy.
    b. The receptionist answered the phone.
    c. No one answered the phone.
    d. The line was busy.

2. What did Gerald do when no one answered the phone at National Shipping?
    a. He called the number again.
    b. He called the operator.
    c. He called directory assistance.
    d. He went back to his other work.

3. Why wasn't Mr. Thomas at work?
    a. He was sick.
    b. It was too early.
    c. He had already left work.
    d. He was on a business trip.

4. An international call is a call to _____.
    a. a local city
    b. another state
    c. another country
    d. a city in another time zone

5. If it is ____ in New York, it is 6 a.m. in California.
    a. 9 a.m.
    b. 9 p.m.
    c. 3 a.m.
    d. 7 p.m.

6. Why does Ms. Minh want to make a conference call?
    a. She needs to talk to several people at the same time.
    b. She needs to talk to someone in another state.
    c. She wants to save money.
    d. She wants to talk to someone in another country.

PRACTICE

A Time your call. Imagine that you are calling from New York. Use the map below to answer the questions. The first one is done for you.

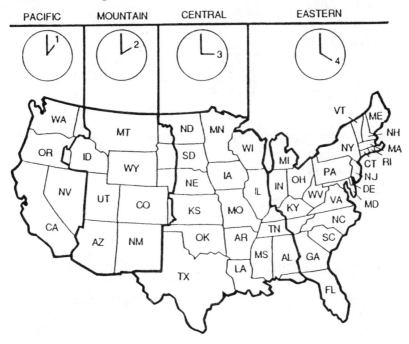

1. You want to call a friend in Oregon. It is now 5 p.m. in New York. What time is it in Oregon?

   It is 2 p.m. in Oregon.

2. You need to place a business call to a company in Ohio. It is 10 a.m. in New York. What time is it in Ohio?

3. You promised to call your friend at 9 a.m. California time. When should you make the call from New York?

4. You want to call a company in Colorado. The company opens at 9 a.m. It is now 11 a.m. in New York. Is it too early to call?

5. You want to call a friend in Texas. She usually goes to bed at 10 p.m. It is now 11:30 p.m. in New York. Is it too late to call her?

B. Choose a word. Choose a word from the list below to complete each sentence. The first one is done for you.

    conference call   international   participants   time zone

1. There were three __**participants**__ in the conference call.

2. Gerald made a call to England. It was an _____ call.

3. Texas is in a different _____ from New York.

4. Ms. Minh made a _____ because she needed to talk to two people at the same time.

C. Choose the type of call. Read about the calls from Gerald's office today. Then decide what type of call it was. Choose from the list below. Write your answer on the blank line. The first one is done for you.

    conference call   local call
    long distance call   international call

__**long distance call**__   1. Ms. Minh called someone in another state.

_____   2. Gerald called the bank in town.

_____   3. A customer in Mexico called Ms. Minh.

_____   4. Ms. Minh talked to Paul Otaro and Jean Readon at the same time.

_____   5. Gerald called a customer in Nevada.

D. Arrange a conference call. Read what Ms. Minh said to Gerald below. Then decide what you would say to Paul Otaro when you call him to set up the conference call. Write your ideas on the blank lines.

Ms. Minh: I want to make a conference call to Paul Otaro and Jean Readon. Paul's number is (504) 554-3392. Jean's number is (304) 548-3301. Set the call up for 3 p.m. today.

_____

_____

_____

_____

UNIT 7

The A, B, Cs of Filing

This unit is about:

- different filing systems
- duties of a file clerk

Think About

Where do you keep your important documents and papers? Are you able to find them easily?
Which papers do you keep and which ones do you throw away? How do you decide?

The A, B, Cs of Filing

Can you believe this? For every twenty pieces of paper in the files of an office, only one is ever retrieved! Because offices store so many papers, the **goal** of a records management system is to keep the papers organized. Then the file clerks will be able to retrieve important information easily.

If you like to keep things organized, you may enjoy working in records management. You must pay attention to detail. You should also have good spelling and typing skills. As more and more records management systems become **automated**, it is also helpful to have some basic computer skills.

Each company has its own system for managing **paperwork**. Every new file clerk has to spend time learning the system used by the company. In a large office, where jobs are more **specialized**, a file clerk may spend most of the day doing the same type of task.

The filing system used by a business is part of its records management plan. Different types of records in a large office may be filed differently. The basic filing systems used in most offices are:

- **ALPHABETIC**—a listing of names in alphabetical order (a, b, c, etc.) Ninety percent of all filing in today's offices uses this system.

        Wong, Anthony K.
        Yasin, Aisha M.
        Yen, Kazuo
        Young, George Allen
        Young, Steven Roy

- **GEOGRAPHIC**—according to place, such as a country, state, or city. This system is often used by sales offices.

> TEXAS (state name)
> Dallas
> Ft. Worth
> Houston   (city names)
> San Antonio
> Waco

- **NUMERIC**—according to an identifying number, such as a customer's account number or social security number. Many businesses with large amounts of paperwork are changing to this system.

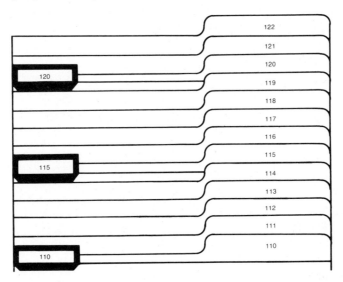

- **SUBJECT**—according to a list of subjects, such as "accounts payable" or "personnel." Small businesses often use this system.

> ACCOUNTING
> Accounts Payable
> Accounts Receivable
> Banking Methods and Procedures
>
> ADVERTISING
> Magazines
> Newspapers
> Radio & TV

Whatever the system, the file clerk's main responsibility is to store company records in the right place. If you are interested in this type of work, there are many opportunities open to you. Who knows? You may come up with an idea for a new filing system. Experience has shown that the best ideas come from the people who do the work.

REVIEW

Choose the best answer. Circle it. Go back to the reading to check your answers. The first one is done for you.

1. Documents, reports, and letters are examples of _____.
    a. filing systems
    (b.) records
    c. management plans
    d. subjects

2. Why do you think so much paperwork is stored away in files?
    a. Because it may be needed at a later date.
    b. Because it creates jobs for file clerks.
    c. Because businesses cannot make decisions.
    d. Because the filing systems are not very good.

3. In a numeric filing system, which file would come first?
    a. 8071
    b. 8170
    c. 8001
    d. 8701

4. Filing according to place is called _____.
    a. geographic
    b. subject
    c. numeric
    d. alphabetic

5. The subject filing system is often used in _____.
    a. government agencies
    b. hospitals
    c. small businesses
    d. radio and television

6. Another title for this unit might be _____.
    a. Numeric Filing Systems
    b. Jobs for File Clerks
    c. Making a Management Plan
    d. Different Filing Systems

PRACTICE

A. Put them in alphabetical order. The accounting department of the Reliance Insurance Company keeps its records in alphabetical order according to company name. Arrange the company names below in alphabetical order. Write your list on the lines at the right. The first one is done for you.

Mountain Lakes Motel	<u>**Anoka Cooperative Dairy**</u>
Ben's Body Shop	_____
Northeast Van Lines	_____
Home & Garden Hardware	_____
Anoka Cooperative Dairy	_____
First State Bank	_____
New Peking Restaurant	_____
Quick Stop Clinic	_____

B. What's your number? Some businesses keep their customer records according to telephone numbers. Choose five names and telephone numbers from your telephone directory or ask five friends. List them below in numeric sequence, starting with the lowest number and ending with the highest.

Number	Name
_____	_____
_____	_____
_____	_____
_____	_____
_____	_____

C. Going places. The sales department of a California computer company uses a geographic filing system to store its records. The records are filed by (1) city and (2) company name. Your supervisor has asked you to put the files on the left in the correct order. Write them in order on the blank lines. The first one is done for you.

Ames Business Supply
Los Angeles

Colonial Gift
San Diego

Choices Gallery
San Francisco

Taylor Rental Center
Bakersville

Wishbasket
San Jose

Serv-Tech
Fresno

Bakersville, Taylor Rental Center

_____

_____

_____

_____

_____

D. What kind of system? Identify the type of filing system—**geographic, numeric,** or **subject**—used in the examples below. Write the name of the system on the blank line. The first one is done for you.

Example	Type of Filing System
1. OFFICE Meetings Memos Procedures Services Space	**Subject**
2. 276-3002 276-3306 276-3812 276-4183 276-4529	_____
3. PHILIPPINES Baguio Batangas Cebu Manila San Pablo	_____

UNIT 8

What's the Password?

This unit is about:

- two kinds of filing systems
- working in a records department

Think About

What kinds of information do you think a hospital has to keep in a filing system? A bank? A department store?

Have you seen someone using a computer in a store? What did they use the computer for?

What's the Password?

George Ferrera works in the office of a large department store. The office uses two types of filing systems: alphabetical and numeric. The employee records are stored alphabetically, by the employee's last name. The customer records, on the other hand, are stored numerically on a computer.

When an employee is hired, George creates a new file. This file stays **active** as long as the employee is with the company. When the employee leaves the company, the file becomes inactive. George stores the active employee files in two five-drawer metal cabinets. These cabinets are **fireproof**. They will not be destroyed even if the building burns down. George is also careful to keep the file drawers locked whenever he leaves the office.

To create a new employee file, George takes an empty folder and types the employee's full name (last name first) on a label. He attaches the label to the tab on the file folder. Then he places the folder in alphabetical order in the filing cabinet.

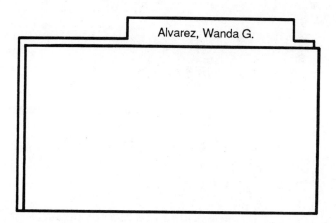

When an employee file becomes inactive, George takes it to the storage room. He puts the file in alphabetical order in a cardboard box. It will stay there for several years before the company destroys it.

Like most modern businesses, the department store also has a **computerized** filing system. This system stores customer information. It keeps records on all customers who apply for charge accounts or use the store's layaway plan. Customers with charge accounts can take things home before paying for them. The layaway plan lets customers pay a little each month. The store keeps the item "on layaway" until the person pays for it.

George does not need a typewriter, filing cabinets, folders, or labels to create files for customers. He simply uses his **computer terminal** to **enter**, or type in, information. Whenever George wants to **access**, or get into, a customer's file, he enters the customer's account number. The customer's file appears on his computer **screen**.

When George wants to get information about a customer, he must first enter a special secret **password**. Only employees who are allowed to see customer information know the password. Using a password is something like locking up a filing cabinet. It keeps the information safe and secure.

At first, George did not like the computerized filing system. He thought it was too difficult. Now that he knows how to use it, he wishes that all the company's records were stored on computer. "Oh, sure, we have problems sometimes," he admits. "But it's easier and faster. I'd hate to go back to the old system now."

REVIEW

Choose the best answer. Circle it. Go back to the reading to check your answers. The first one is done for you.

1. Which records does George store alphabetically?
    a. inactive customer files only
    b. active customer files only
    (c.) all employee records
    d. customer financial information

2. George stores the active employee files in _____.
    a. filing cabinets
    b. a central computer
    c. cardboard boxes
    d. a computer terminal

3. When George enters information into the computer, he _____.
    a. retrieves it
    b. types it in
    c. files it alphabetically
    d. stores it

4. Which of the following statements is true?
    a. Anyone can access customer files.
    b. Only George can access customer files.
    c. Some employees can access customer files.
    d. Customer files are protected from all employees by a password.

5. How does George feel about the computerized filing system?
    a. He does not like it very much.
    b. He has had a lot of trouble with this system.
    c. George now prefers this system to the old one.
    d. George thinks this system is very slow.

6. Another title for this unit could be _____.
    a. Two Ways to File Important Information
    b. Where to Put Active Employee Files
    c. Using a Computer
    d. Accessing Customer Information

PRACTICE

A. Label the files. Make a file for each of the people below. Write the name of the person on the file tab. Write the last name, then a comma, then the first name. The first one is done for you.

John Martin
Mary James
Jean Mundo
Kevin Hines
Robert Cresta
Jeff C. Murphy

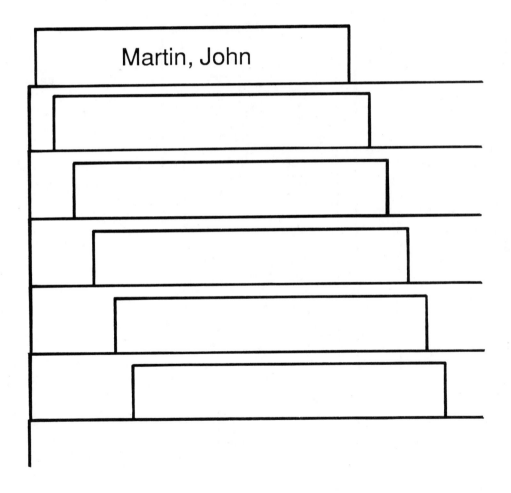

B. Which drawer are they in? The labels on the front of this filing cabinet show which files are stored in each drawer. Decide where you would find the files of the employees listed below. Remember that the files are in alphabetical order according to the employee's last name. Write the names of the employees next to the drawer which holds their file. An example is provided for you.

      Ruen, Sam An   Adams, David M.
      Zhang, Xia   Callas, Victoria E.
      Lyndon, James   McGuire, Silvia J
      Wallace, Ruth N.   Nguyen, Tanh Thi

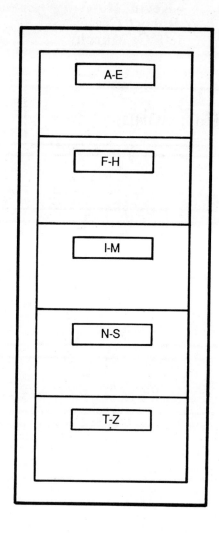

McGuire, Silvia J

UNIT 9

Mail It

This unit is about:

- services of the post office
- working in the post office

Think About

Do you know anyone who works in the post office?
Would you like to work in the post office? Why or Why not?

Mail It

Frank always laughs to himself when someone walks up to his window at the post office and asks, "When will this letter get there?"

"If they only knew how many different ways there are to mail that letter!" he says. "And it seems that every week, they tell us about a new type of mailing. Mailing a letter does not mean just licking a stamp and sticking it on an envelope. You have to know your choices and decide on the best one for your letter."

According to Frank, **first-class** mail is still the most popular way to send things. First-class letters and postcards must weigh 12 ounces or less. Most of the stamps that Frank sells are first-class postage stamps. People who use first-class mail want their letters to arrive quickly.

Priority mail is first-class mail for packages that weigh between twelve ounces and seventy pounds. People use priority mail when they want their packages to arrive quickly. Priority mail will also get a letter to its destination a little faster than regular first-class mail.

People don't come up to Frank's window and ask to mail things second-class. Companies use this class of mail to send newspapers and magazines.

On the other hand, Frank handles a lot of third-class mail or **bulk business mail**. Most people use this class of mail to send a large quantity of letters or packages. If they are sending 200 or more pieces of mail, the post office charges a lower bulk rate. The sender can also save money by **presorting** the pieces by ZIP Code. Presorting—grouping the mail of the same ZIP Code before taking it to the post office—makes Frank's job much easier.

Frank also handles a lot of **fourth-class mail**, or parcel post. Fourth-class mail is for packages of a certain size which weigh between 16 ounces and 70 pounds. This is a slower way to send packages than priority mail.

Frank says that these days he is handling more **express mail**. This is a special fast service. Express mail can be delivered either the same day that it is mailed or the day after. This costs more, but it is useful when someone really needs to send something fast. The other day Frank helped a woman who really needed express mail. She had to send a job application. The **deadline** for receipt of the application was the next day. So, she sent the application by express mail next day service. She paid more for the express delivery, but it may have gotten her the job.

The post office has a number of other services. Frank says that one commonly used service is **certified** mail. This provides the sender with a mailing receipt and a record of delivery. People send important business letters, bills, or certificates by certified mail. Many people use certified mail to prove that they sent a letter or document.

When people mail something of value, they often **insure** it. They can insure third- and fourth-class mail for up to $400. When Frank handles insured mail, he prepares a receipt, stamps the mail *INSURED*, and writes the receipt number on the package. If the post office loses or damages the mail, it will pay the sender the value of the item, up to the amount of insurance.

With all the ways to mail things, Frank's job is anything but boring. "Working at the post office is a lot more than selling stamps," he says.

REVIEW

Choose the best answer. Circle it. Go back to the reading to check your answers. The first one is done for you.

1. From the reading, you can guess that _____.
    a. Frank is a customer at the post office
    b. Frank has worked at the post office for 10 years
    (c.) Frank is a post office employee
    d. Frank does not like his job

2. Most magazines and newspapers are sent by _____.
    a. first-class mail
    b. second-class mail
    c. third-class mail
    d. fourth-class mail

3. Bulk is another word for _____.
    a. mail
    b. airmail
    c. express
    d. large quantity

4. If you wanted a letter to arrive the next day, you would use _____.
    a. certified mail
    b. express mail
    c. first-class mail
    d. insured mail

5. You must pay a bill by mail. You want to be sure that your payment arrives. How would you mail it?
    a. certified mail
    b. bulk business mail
    c. parcel post
    d. priority mail

6. Another title for this unit could be _____.
    a. Bulk Business Mail
    b. Insuring Your Packages
    c. Working at the Post Office
    d. Services of the Post Office

PRACTICE

A. What is the definition? Read the words in column A. Then choose the correct definition for each word from column B. Write the letter of the definition on the blank line. The first one is done for you.

A		B	
_e_	1. insured mail	a.	a service that provides a record of delivery
___	2. certified mail	b.	put in order before mailing
___	3. deadline	c.	large mailings
___	4. bulk mail	d.	the time when something is due
___	5. presorted mail	e.	mail whose value is protected up to $400

B. Fill in the chart. Use the information in the reading to fill in the chart below. Explain what each class of mail is used for. Write the information in the box. The first one is done for you.

Class of Mail	Used for
First-class	mail that weighs 12 ounces or less
Priority	
Second-class	
Third-class	
Fourth-class	
Express	

C. How did they send it? Anne and George Seiler own a small construction company. The list below shows the mail they sent out today. Decide how they sent each item. Write your answers on the blank lines. The first one is done for you.

first-class   second-class   third-class   fourth-class
express   insured   certified

1. 200 presorted postcards
   telling about their business   ___third-class mail___

2. the electricity bill   _____

3. a letter asking for
   product information   _____

4. a letter that must
   arrive the next day   _____

5. a 20-pound package
   worth $100.00, no rush   _____

6. 100 bills to customers   _____

7. a package with valuable
   drawings inside, no rush   _____

8. their son's birth
   certificate   _____

D. How do you want to send it? Decide how you would send each of the items below. Choose **certified** or **insured**. Put a checkmark in the correct column. The first one is done for you.

	certified	insured
1. birth certificate	√	
2. wedding gift		
3. passport		
4. tax payment		
5. birthday present		

UNIT 10

Preparing Outgoing Mail

This unit is about:

- sending mail from an office
- new ways to send things

Think About

What businesses do you receive mail from?
Would you like to work in the mailroom of a business? Why or why not?

Preparing Outgoing Mail

People who handle the mail in offices have to be mailing experts. After working in the mailroom of a computer company for 3 years, Dick Stevens knows a lot about the mail. People in all departments of the company depend on Dick. Here are some of the things Dick has to do on a typical day.

9:00 a.m.—Dick has just finished his coffee when one of the secretaries comes in with a rush mailing. It is a 100-page report that must get to California before the end of the day. Dick's company is in New York. The secretary tells Dick that cost is not important. Dick sees only one way: express mail same day service. He fills out a slip with the destination, return address, and phone numbers. He places the report in an express mail envelope and gives it to one of his assistants to take to the express mail office at the airport. There it will be put on an airplane. It is sure to get to the California office today.

9:30 a.m.—Dick is given a bulk mailing of 500 pieces. There is no big rush on this mailing. Dick knows that it should go by third-class bulk rate. It is the least expensive way to send it. In order to get the cheap rate, Dick must presort the mailing by ZIP Code.

1:00 p.m.—After lunch, Dick is asked to send an important document on the **facsimile machine** or **fax**. The fax machine is a long-distance **copier**. It can send a perfect copy of Dick's document through the telephone lines to another fax machine at a distant location. Faxing is the quickest way to send a document. Faxing one page takes just a little longer than making a long distance telephone call.

To "fax a document," Dick puts the original document into the fax machine. Then he calls the number of the receiving fax machine. The fax machine beeps a few times. In a few seconds a copy of the document appears on the receiving fax machine. Sometimes Dick has to send things to other countries. He enjoys the thought that the information on the paper can travel so far in a few seconds.

4:00 p.m.—The last task of Dick's workday is to prepare a package of computer parts for mailing. There is no rush on the package; Dick decides to send it parcel post. He knows that the package can measure up to 108 inches in **combined** length and **girth**. The girth is the distance around the parcel at its thickest part. Since the parts are valuable, Dick must also remember to insure the package.

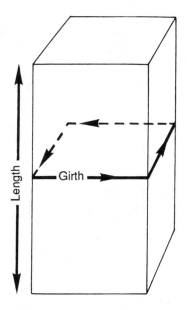

Length + Girth = Package Size

Dick wraps the items individually and places them in a box of the correct size. He puts a packing list inside the box. The packing list contains a list of the parcel's contents and the sender's and receiver's addresses. Dick seals the box with heavy tape, **affixes** a mailing label, and stamps the package *FRAGILE*. Then the package is ready to send out.

5:00 p.m.—When the package is ready, Dick calls it a day. He leaves work knowing he has sent out the company's mail in the safest and quickest way possible.

REVIEW

Choose the best answer. Circle it. Go back to the reading to check your answers. The first one is done for you.

1. Someone who works in an office mailroom must _____.
    a. know about the different ways to mail things
    b. know how to take phone messages
    c. write and type many letters
    d. keep customer files

2. Why did Dick use express mail same day service to mail the report?
    a. Because it was very heavy.
    b. Because he wasn't busy.
    c. Because the California office needed it right away.
    d. Because it was the cheapest way to mail the report.

3. Dick decided to send the 500-piece mailing by third-class bulk rate because it was _____.
    a. the fastest way to send it
    b. the least expensive way to send it
    c. the easiest way to send it
    d. the safest way to send it

4. Why did Dick presort the bulk mailing by ZIP Code?
    a. The post office only accepts presorted mail.
    b. He wanted to get the cheaper rate.
    c. He wanted the mailing to arrive faster.
    d. He wanted the more expensive rate.

5. The facsimile machine, or fax, is a _____.
    a. class of mailing
    b. telephone
    c. kind of stamp
    d. long distance copier

6. Another title for this unit could be _____.
    a. How to Measure Packages
    b. Dick Stevens
    c. Working in a Mailroom
    d. Using the Fax Machine

PRACTICE

A. Group the ZIP Codes. Look at the list of ZIP Codes below. Group them according to the first three digits. Write the correct ZIP code in each column. The first one is done for you.

02115	02291	02344	02131
02334	02256	02152	02380
02211	02112	02246	02377

021   **022**   **023**

_02115_   _____   _____

_____   _____   _____

_____   _____   _____

_____   _____   _____

B. What's the answer? Use the information in the reading to answer the questions. Write your answers on the blank lines. The first one is done for you.

1. How does Dick send the 100-page report?

   He sends it express mail same day service.

2. Why does Dick presort the bulk mailing?

   _____

3. What does Dick use the telephone for?

   _____

4. How does Dick decide to mail the package?

   _____

5. What does Dick affix to the package?

   _____

C. Fill out a packing list. Use the information below to fill out the packing list. The list is started for you.

Sender: Ivan Clothing Co.
P.O. Box 52
Miami, FL 39402

Addressee: Linda Larson
1821 Mayfair Ave.
Costa Mesa, CA 98432

Contents:
1 girls' sweatshirt
2 pairs of boys' jeans
1 women's turtleneck sweater
1 pair men's gloves
1 pair women's gloves

Ivan Clothing Co.
P.O. Box 52
Miami, FL 39402

PACKING LIST
*Thank You For
Your Order*

S
O
L _____
D
   _____
T
O _____

Quantity Shipped	Description
1	Girls' sweatshirt

D. Measure the parcels. Look at the measurements of the parcels below. Fill in the blanks with the length and girth. Then add the numbers together to find the total size. The first one is done for you.

1.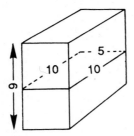

length   __9"__

girth   __30"__

total size   __39"__

2.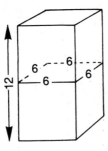

length _____

girth _____

total size _____

3.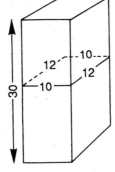

length _____

girth _____

total size _____

4.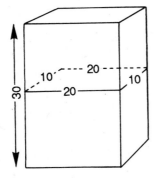

length _____

girth _____

total size _____

UNIT 11

From Words To Letters

This unit is about:

- different types of business letters
- putting information into letters

Think About

Who do you think does most of the letter writing in an office? What kinds of letters do you think they write?

From Words To Letters

Marla Thomas is a **correspondence** secretary for a large wallpaper business. The business sells wallpaper to hotels and offices. Marla's main responsibility is to prepare office documents. To qualify for this job, Marla had to have excellent typing, spelling, and letter writing skills.

Marla's employer, Janine Munoz, often asks her to write letters. Ms. Munoz tells Marla what information the letter must contain. Marla then takes this information and writes the letter using her own words.

Marla follows the same writing steps no matter what kind of letter she is writing. Before she starts writing, Marla always asks herself this question: What is the main purpose of this letter? On a note pad, Marla lists the important information to include in the letter. Then she decides on the best order for the information. Once this is done, she begins to write the letter.

On her word processor, Marla types a **first draft** of the letter. She follows these rules as she writes:

1. <u>Be complete</u>. Use all the information you have listed.

2. <u>Be clear</u>. Say your ideas simply. Use short sentences.

3. **Be polite**. Use "please" with requests. Say "thank you" for things that people have done for you or your employer.

4. **Be concise**. Include only the most necessary information. Check that every word you use is necessary to get your message across in a polite way.

Marla reads the first draft of the letter and **edits** it. Editing consists of making revisions, or changes, to the first draft of a document. Marla takes out a few unnecessary words and corrects several spelling mistakes. When Marla thinks the letter is just right, she puts the company's **letterhead stationery** into the printer. This special paper has the company's name and address at the top. Marla types the **command** to print and within seconds her letter comes out of the printer. She reads it over again to make sure there are no mistakes. This is what Marla's finished letter looks like:

GREER WALLPAPER CO.
203 Seventh Avenue
New York, NY 10012

April 10, 1991

Sherman Interiors Inc.
210 Long Island Parkway
Syosset, NY 10293

Dear Mr. Kumar:

The box of paper samples that you sent arrived today. Thank you for sending the samples so quickly. Ms. Munoz will be away from the office next week, but she will get in touch with you as soon as she returns.

Sincerely,

Marla Thomas

Marla Thomas
Correspondence Secretary

This type of letter is called an **acknowledgement letter**; it says that something was received. Marla writes many other kinds of letters too. But no matter which kind of letter she writes, Marla always follows the same writing steps.

REVIEW

Choose the best answer. Circle it. Go back to the reading to check your answers. The first one is done for you.

1. Marla's duties include _____.
    a. hiring employees
    (b.) writing letters
    c. giving the employer general information for writing letters
    d. fixing office equipment

2. What does Marla do with the first draft of her letter?
    a. She mails it.
    b. She prints it out.
    c. She checks it and makes some changes.
    d. She gives it to Ms. Munoz to check.

3. The opposite meaning of concise is _____.
    a. wordy
    b. exact
    c. short
    d. polite

4. Marla prints the final copy of the letter on _____.
    a. scrap paper
    b. letterhead stationery
    c. a blank sheet of regular paper
    d. an envelope

5. Why do you think it is important to edit a letter?
    a. It's important to find any mistakes.
    b. It helps you to relax.
    c. It takes a lot of time.
    d. It's important to make the letter longer.

6. Another title for this unit could be _____.
    a. Writing a Thank You Letter
    b. Asking for Payment
    c. The Steps in Writing a Business Letter
    d. Different Kinds of Business Letters

PRACTICE

A Using polite expressions. Read the sentences below. Then rewrite them using polite expressions such as *please, thank you, would you mind*. The first one is done for you.

1. Send the package.

   Please send the package.

2. Where is your payment?

   _____

3. Call Mr. Torres on Thursday.

   _____

4. You referred a client to us.

   _____

5. Send the check by Friday.

   _____

6. We want to see samples of your product.

   _____

B. What is the definition? Match the words in List A with the definitions in List B. The first one is done for you.

	A		B
e	1. acknowledgement letter	a.	paper for business letters
___	2. purpose	b.	reason for doing something
___	3. letterhead stationery	c.	without extra words
___	4. concise	d.	communication by letters
___	5. correspondence	e.	written statement that something was received

C. Be concise. The sentences below are too wordy. Cross out the unnecessary words. Change some words if necessary. Then, rewrite your new sentence on the blank line. The first one is done for you.

1. We were certainly pleased to receive your beautiful package.

   We were pleased to receive your package.

2. We here are looking forward very much to your visit soon next week.

   _____

3. Here in this letter is enclosed a check for the services that you have provided.

   _____

4. We at Hansen Inc. are not at all pleased with the quality of the goods that your company has sent us by mail.

   _____

5. Would you mind at all if we do not send the goods that you ordered until July 5th because Ms. Munoz is going to a wedding the day before.

   _____

6. We heard that you are having some business problems so we would like you to send us a cash payment for our services immediately.

   _____

D. Write a letter. Use the general ideas below to write a letter. Make a first draft of the letter on a separate piece of paper. Then rewrite your letter on a clean sheet of paper.

- your company received a box of books that you ordered
- you received the books on October 19th
- the books were in good condition
- you want to thank Owl Books, the company that sent the books
- you received the books very quickly

UNIT 12

It's All in the Details

This unit is about:

- checking letters for mistakes
- reading and following directions

Think About

When you write a letter, do you check it over before you mail it? What would you think if you received a business letter with lots of mistakes in it?

It's All in the Details

The work that a secretary does can help or hurt a company's **image**. A business letter with lots of mistakes might cause a customer to form a bad **opinion** of that company. Paying attention to the little things—the overall **appearance** of the letter, the spelling and grammar, even the way the letter is folded—all add up to creating a **professional** image.

It is always important to pay attention to detail. When you choose the paper for a letter, choose clean sheets of paper. Type the business letter neatly and make sure the parts of the letter are placed correctly on the page. The letter should look neither empty nor crowded with information.

After you have typed and edited the letter, there is still important work to do. **Proofreading** is a necessary step in the business letter writing process. Proofreading means reading over something to check for mistakes. The mistakes could be simple typing or spelling errors. It is also important to check for grammar or **punctuation** mistakes. For example, after typing a letter, you might have a **paragraph** like this:

> We are now offering all of our customets a twenty persent discount on all items. This offer will lasted until the 18th of Januaty 1991. If you are interested, please call our customer service offfice as soon as possible. Thank you for doing business with us

Proofreading the paragraph shows that there are six mistakes. Can you find them? The corrected paragraph is shown below.

> We are now offering all of our customers a twenty percent discount on all items. This offer will last until the 18th of January 1991. If you are interested, please call our customer service office as soon as possible. Thank you for doing business with us.

Once you have typed, proofread, corrected, and signed the letter, it is ready to go in an envelope. This is another point in the process when it is important to pay attention to detail. A carefully folded business letter presents a professional image. The picture below shows the correct way to fold a business letter.

How To Fold A Letter (No. 10 envelope)

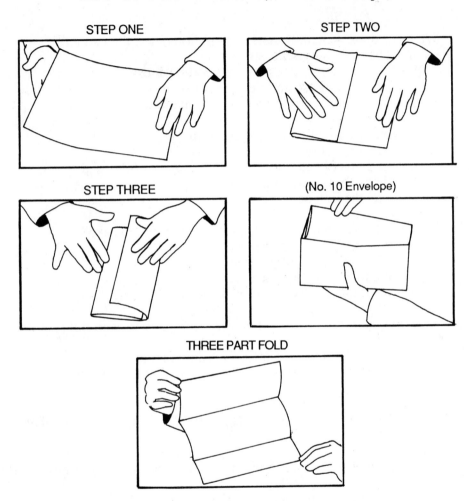

The letter you send says something about the company you work for. If you want people to have a good opinion of the company, your letter must present a professional image. You can also take pride in the knowledge that you have done your work well.

REVIEW

Choose the best answer. Circle it. Go back to the reading to check your answers. The first one is done for you.

1. Which of these sentences states an opinion rather than a fact?
    a. That company sells wallpaper.
    (b.) That company does not do good business.
    c. There are six secretaries in her office.
    d. She uses a word processor to write letters.

2. When you proofread a letter, you should _____.
    a. read it quickly
    b. read it very carefully
    c. check for punctuation only
    d. read the first paragraph only

3. Which of these sentences contains a punctuation mistake?
    a. We sent your package last week.
    b. We received your package
    c. We received your package.
    d. We didn't receive your package.

4. Why do you think it is important for a company to send out professional letters?
    a. It costs less to produce professional letters.
    b. The company wants people to think that it does good business.
    c. The company wants to spend more on the letters.
    d. The company wants to make people believe something that is not true.

5. Why do you think it is important to fold a business letter as described in the reading?
    a. It takes less time to fold it this way.
    b. The letter cannot be read if it is folded another way.
    c. It will fit neatly into a business envelope.
    d. The post office will not deliver letters folded in other ways.

6. Another title for this unit could be _____.
    a. The Parts of a Business Letter
    b. Proofreading a Paragraph
    c. Writing A Professional Business Letter
    d. Getting To Know Your Customers

PRACTICE

A Find the errors. Each of the sentences below has one or more spelling or typing errors. Find the errors and underline them. Then, rewrite the sentence on the blank line. The first one is done for you.

1. Our office Christmas <u>patty</u> will be <u>one</u> December 15th.

    <u>**Our office Christmas party will be on December 15th.**</u>

2. We value al our customers' business.

    _____

3. We look fowrard to hearing from yu.

    _____

4. All employes must attend the meetting on Friday.

    _____

5. This year, we hvae had a rise in sales in all departments.

    _____

B. Correct the sentences. Each of the sentences below has a punctuation mistake. Read the sentences and add the necessary punctuation marks. Cross out any unnecessary punctuation marks.

1. The restroom is down the hall and to the right
2. He is going to write, a letter to his family.
3. We got in the car and, drove to the office.
4. Where did you leave your umbrella?.

5. Its important to use the dictionary to check the spelling of new words.

6. There are some letters in the mailbox:

7. This package is heavier than that one

8. It's a good idea to take a break from proofreading when youre tired.

9. They took their coffee break at 3:00

10. The letter fell, out of the envelope.

C. Practice folding a letter. Find the directions for folding a business letter in the reading. Fold a piece of blank paper following the directions. Then, follow the directions below for a smaller, number 6 envelope.

How To Fold A Letter (No. 6 Envelope)

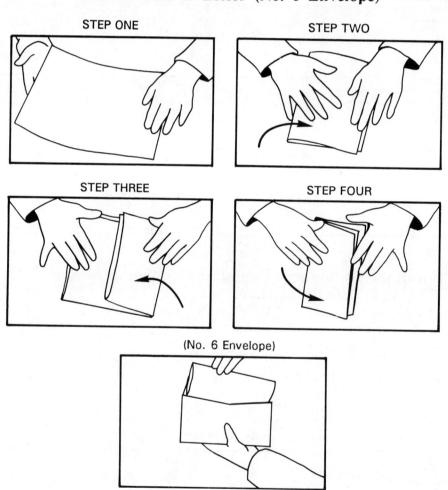

74

UNIT 13

Getting the Message

This unit is about:

- sending messages within an office
- writing memos

Think About

Besides talking, how do you send messages to the people you live with?

How do you think people who work in different departments of an office send messages to each other?

Getting the Message

In addition to sending letters to people outside of the business, Marla sends messages to people inside the office. She sometimes has to leave informal notes or instructions for her employer, Ms. Munoz. Sometimes she has to send messages from Ms. Munoz to people in other departments.

Sometimes Marla has to remind Ms. Munoz to sign a letter. Sometimes she has a question about a letter or form. For these informal messages, Marla uses special note paper that is sticky on the back. These notes **adhere**, or stick, to other pieces of paper, but they are easy to remove too.

The most common type of office message that Marla writes is a **memorandum** or **memo**. Most memos deal with daily business matters in the office. They carry messages to people in different departments of the office. For example, one of the supervisors might send a memo to remind people about a meeting.

The **style** of a memo depends on the company. Most memos include the name of the receiver, the sender, the date, the subject, and the body or main message. When Marla writes a memo, she uses a company form. She can type the memo on her computer and then print it on the form. A typical memo that Marla wrote for Ms. Munoz is shown below.

GREER WALLPAPER CO.
Interoffice Memorandum

TO: Jane Fox, Accounts Supervisor

FROM: Janine Munoz, President

DATE: September 12, 1991

SUBJECT: Jaffa Account

Please remind the staff in your department that the Jaffa account will be reviewed on Friday.

I will give you a full report of your work on Monday before noon.

mt

For this memo, Marla typed the names of the receiver and sender. She did not use personal titles such as *Mr.* or *Ms.*, but she did include each person's official title. For example, after Janine Munoz, she wrote *President*. Because Marla wrote the memo for Ms. Munoz, she added her own initials in **lower case** letters at the bottom.

When Marla sends a memo to someone in another department, she places the memo in an **interoffice envelope**. These large envelopes are useful because they can be used over and over again. First Marla crosses out the last name on the envelope. Then she writes the name and department of the person to whom she is sending the memo.

INTEROFFICE CORRESPONDENCE			
TO	DEPT.	TO	DEPT.
~~Barbara N.~~	~~Edit.~~		
~~Karen K.~~	~~Art~~		
~~Nancy L.~~	~~HR~~		
Mike N.	Mfg.		

There are many different ways to communicate with people inside the office. Writing a memo is one good way to send important information. When you put the information in writing, you can be sure that everyone will get the message.

REVIEW

Choose the best answer. Circle it. Go back to the reading to check your answers. The first one is done for you.

1. Another word for adhere is _____.
   a. stick *(circled)*
   b. write
   c. memorandum
   d. communicate

2. A memorandum includes the name of the receiver, sender, date and _____.
   a. address of sender
   b. address of receiver
   c. exact time of writing
   d. subject

3. Why do you think the company has a form for memos?
   a. It is cheaper.
   b. The company does not want to waste paper.
   c. It saves time.
   d. It takes more time to use a form.

4. Why does Marla put her initials at the bottom of the memo?
   a. Because Ms. Munoz wrote the memo.
   b. Because Marla wrote the memo for Ms. Munoz.
   c. Because the memo was for Marla.
   d. Because she was the subject of the memo.

5. Marla uses an interoffice envelope _____.
   a. to send express mail
   b. to send memos to other departments
   c. to send formal letters to customers
   d. to send mail out of the office

6. Another title for this unit could be _____.
   a. How to Use an Interoffice Envelope
   b. Interoffice Communication
   c. How to Write a Memo
   d. The Different Ways to Write a Memo

PRACTICE

A. Proofread the memo. There are five mistakes in the memo below. Underline the spelling mistakes. Add the missing punctuation marks. An example is provided for you.

GREER WALLPAPER CO.
Interoffice Memorandum

TO: Jane Fox, Accounts Sup<u>ir</u>visor

FROM: Janine Munoz President

DATE: September 15 1991

SUBJECT: Merrill Acount

Please remind the staff in your department that the Merrill account will be revewed on Friday

I will give a full report on the budget at that time.

mt

B. Proofread the addresses. Read each of the addresses on the left. Then check the addresses on the right. Find the mistake in each typed address. Underline it. The first one is done for you.

1. *Mr. Steven Spender*　　　　Mr. Steven Spender
   32 Center Street　　　　　32 <u>Centr</u> Street
   Omaha, NE 68144-3155　　Omaha, NE 68144-3155

2. *Farfel Design Co.*　　　　　Farfel Design Col
   10029 Buena Vista　　　　10029 Buena Vista
   Los Angeles, CA 98221　　Los Angeles, CA 98221

79

3. *General Manufacturing Co.* General Manufacturing Co.
   5738 Western Drive 5738 Western Drive
   St. Paul, MN 55102 St. Pal, MN 55102

4. *Ms. Francin Jones* Ms. Francin Jones
   53 Pine Street 53 Pine Street
   Pontiac, MI 48055 Pontiac, MI 48054

5. *Dr. George Franklin* Dr. George Franklin
   288 State Street 288 State Street
   Troy, NY 12210 Troy, NU 12210

C. Write a memorandum. Use the general ideas below to write a memo to a friend. Be sure to proofread your memo.

<u>General Ideas</u>
you are having an office party for someone's birthday
you want people to be in your office at 2:30 on Friday
you want it to be a secret

Interoffice Memorandum

TO:

FROM:

DATE:

SUBJECT:

_____
_____
_____
_____
_____
_____
_____

UNIT 14

The Electronic Office

This unit is about:

- computers in the workplace
- the electronic office

Think About

Think of an office you have visited. What was it like? What kinds of machines and furniture did you see?
How do you think today's office is different from an office twentyfive years ago?

The Electronic Office

To get an **entry-level** position in an office twenty-five years ago, you probably needed basic typing and filing skills. You might have seen typewriters, adding machines, and dozens of filing cabinets in the office. The office workers' desks were probably lined up in straight rows. The supervisors probably worked in offices of their own. You would have been surprised at how much noise the typewriters made. You might have been amazed at how often the office workers had to leave their desks to deliver papers, file documents, or complete other tasks.

The skills needed in an office twenty-five years ago are still useful today. However, today's office worker must have other kinds of training too. In many offices there are no typewriters and only a few filing cabinets. Employee **workstations** may be arranged around the manager or supervisor's office. At each workstation, an employee works at a personal computer.

Today the computer is an important tool for communicating and managing information. As you already know, employees can use computers to store information and write letters. They can also use computers to send messages and manage payrolls.

Marla, the correspondence secretary at Greer Wallpaper Company, has a computer at her workstation. She uses the computer to write letters and to update files. To type a letter, Marla uses a **keyboard** which is similar to the keys on a typewriter. The words she types appear immediately on the computer screen. Marla can read her words on the screen and then make corrections and changes. For example, she can **delete**, or take out, a word very quickly. She can correct a spelling mistake in seconds. When Marla wants a **hard copy** of her letter, she types in a special command. The printer which is connected to her computer quickly prints out a copy of her letter.

In order to write letters on the computer, Marla must use computer **software**. Software is a set of instructions which tell the computer how to do a job. There are many different kinds of software, but Marla can do most of her work with word processing software.

At the end of the day, Marla makes a copy of everything she wrote on the computer. In case there is a problem with the computer, she wants to have a record of her work. To make a copy, Marla puts a **disk** into the computer. Then she gives the command for copying information. Marla can then take out the disk and store it in a safe place.

Writing letters is much easier on a computer. If you already know how to type, it should be easy for you to learn the keyboarding skills you need to use the word processing software.

REVIEW

Choose the best answer. Circle it. Go back to the reading to check your answers. The first one is done for you.

1. The skills needed by an office worker 25 years ago are _____.
    a. not needed now
    b. unhelpful
    c. useless now
    ⓓ. still useful

2. Which person would apply for an entry-level position?
    a. someone who is applying for his or her first job
    b. someone who has worked for several years
    c. someone who has years of experience
    d. someone who wants to be a supervisor

3. When might you use word processing software?
    a. to store disks
    b. to hand-write forms
    c. to write letters
    d. to organize your workstation

4. Marla can read the letter on _____.
    a. the computer screen
    b. the keyboard
    c. the software
    d. the command

5. Another word for delete is _____.
    a. type in
    b. remove
    c. copy
    d. command

6. A letter on company stationery is an example of _____.
    a. a hard copy
    b. a disk
    c. software
    d. a workstation

PRACTICE

A Name the parts. The drawing below shows the main parts of a personal computer. Label the **keyboard,** the **screen,** and the **printer**. The first one is done for you.

1. __printer__   2. _____   3. _____

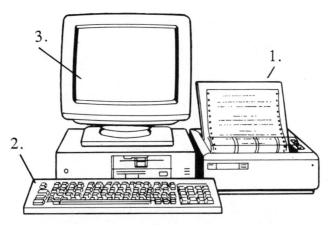

B. Choose a word. Use one of the words below to complete the sentences. The first one is done for you.

    delete   disk   entry-level   hard copy
    keyboard   screen   software   workstation

1. Marla makes a copy of her work on another __disk__ .

2. You can read the information on the _____ before you print it out.

3. You can _____ words easily on a computer.

4. Marla uses a _____ to type in information.

5. A printer makes a _____ of your work.

6. Because he does not have much work experience, he is going to take an _____ position.

7. He spends most of the day at his own _____ .

8. _____ is a set of instructions for a computer.

C. Then and now. Compare an office worker's job 25 years ago with the job of a worker in a modern electronic office. Read each sentence below. Then write a sentence that describes a difference. The first one is done for you.

1. Twenty-five years ago an office worker needed to have good typing skills.

    An office worker today needs word processing skills.

2. The desks were arranged in rows, one behind the other.

    _____

    _____

3. All information was stored in filing cabinets.

    _____

    _____

4. Office workers carried messages from one part of the office to another.

    _____

    _____

D. What's your opinion? In the electronic office, workers have to learn new skills in order to keep up with changing technology. What can companies do to help their employees keep up with new technology? Write your ideas on the lines below. An example is given for you.

   Companies can provide books and magazines that give

   information on changes in office technology.

   _____

   _____

   _____

   _____

   _____

   _____

UNIT 15

In Good Time

This unit is about:

- managing your time at work
- organizing your workplace

Think About

Think about the saying "Time is money." When is it true?
Think of some tasks that you do not enjoy doing. How could you do these tasks faster?

In Good Time

People often say that time is money. This is especially true for office workers. Employees who manage their time well are worth more to the company. They are more likely to get **pay raises.** They are also more likely to be **promoted**, or moved up in the company.

Read the stories below about two office workers, Keith and John. Compare how these two employees manage their time.

KEITH

Keith usually gets to work on time or just a few minutes late. As soon as he sits down at his workstation, he starts right to work. Every morning there is a big pile of notes and documents on his desk from the day before. He turns on his personal computer and picks up the paper on top of the pile. He reads it and begins to key in the information. The telephone rings. The supervisor wants to know what happened to the customer files she asked for yesterday. She says she sent him a message marked "**URGENT**." Keith looks through the pile of papers but he can't find the message. At quitting time, Keith is still working on the same pile. He hasn't had time to look at any new work orders or messages. Exhausted, he turns off his computer and goes home.

> ## JOHN
>
> John usually arrives at his workstation a few minutes early. Before he turns on his computer, he takes a few minutes to plan the day. He looks at his IN basket to check for urgent messages or letters. He makes a note to take care of these first. Then he looks at his calendar to see if he has any meetings or appointments. Finally, he makes a note of the routine tasks he has to do. He decides how much time he will need for each one. Then he turns on his computer and begins to work. At the end of the day, John stops a few minutes before quitting time to organize his desk and put away his work.

Keith and John are both hard workers, but John is more organized. His supervisor knows that she can depend on him to do the work on time. Here are some tips from John for getting things done in good time.

- Always arrive at work on time. If possible, get there a few minutes early so that you get ready for the day.

- Write the major tasks of the day on a note pad. List the most urgent things first. Leave the less important tasks for later in the day. **Estimate** the amount of time it will take you to do each job.

- Get ready for each job before you start it. Take out the supplies you will need. It takes more time to stop in the middle of a job to look for something than it does to take it out before.

- Avoid chatting for long periods of time with **coworkers** in the office or with friends on the telephone. This causes loss of time and may disturb other employees.

- Stop in time to clear your desk or workstation. Put all papers, documents, and supplies away so that you can find them easily in the morning. Make sure that all electrical equipment is turned off.

Keith and John have different working styles. John, however, can get more work done because he is organized. If you had to promote one of these people, whom would you choose?

REVIEW

Choose the best answer. Circle it. Go back to the reading to check your answers. The first one is done for you.

1. "Time is money" suggests that workers should not _____.
    a. get raises
    b. enjoy their work
    c. manage their time well
    ⓓ. waste time

2. Keith may not get a promotion because he is _____.
    a. lazy
    b. disorganized
    c. always late
    d. unable to use a computer

3. John takes some time at the end of the day to _____.
    a. relax
    b. chat
    c. put things away
    d. make a list

4. A message marked "URGENT" should be _____.
    a. taken care of first
    b. put aside until later
    c. filed away
    d. keyed into the computer

5. John's tips can help you _____.
    a. relax
    b. manage your time
    c. get along with other workers
    d. learn how to use a computer

6. Another title for this unit could be _____.
    a. Getting a Pay Raise
    b. Managing Your Time at Work
    c. The Problem with Keith
    d. Organizing Your Papers

PRACTICE

A   How does John spend his working day? The chart below shows how John usually spends his day in the office. Use the information in the chart to complete the paragraph. Write a word or number in each space. The first one is done for you.

JOHN'S DAY

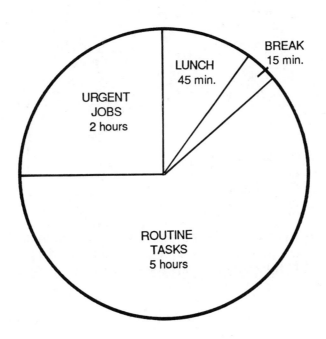

John works from 9:00 in the morning until 5:00 in the afternoon. He takes ____45____ minutes for lunch, and he has a 15-minute break in the late morning. He spends _____ hours a day at his workstation. He always uses time during the day to _____ his time and organize his work. In the morning, he does the _____ jobs first. This usually takes about _____ hours. Then, for the rest of the day, he works on _____ tasks such as filing, opening mail, and writing reports that are not marked "urgent."

B. How much time does it take? Different people take different amounts of time to do certain tasks. To organize your time well, it is important to know how long it takes to do things. Estimate the amount of time it usually takes you to do the following tasks. Write your answers in minutes or hours. Then compare your answers with a friend's. Remember that faster does not always mean better.

How long does it take you to...?

1. cook a simple meal   _____
2. write a letter   _____
3. get dressed   _____
4. make a sandwich   _____
5. pay a bill   _____
6. take a bath   _____
7. eat lunch   _____

C. Put them in order. If you followed John's advice, how would you organize your day? Put the following tasks and activities in order (1, 2, 3, etc.). Go back to the reading if you need help. The first one is done for you.

_____ Clear desk or workstation. Put away supplies.

_____ List the major tasks of the day.

__1__ Arrive at work on time or a few minutes early.

_____ Do the jobs marked "urgent" or "important."

_____ Go home.

_____ Make sure all electrical equipment is off.

_____ Do the routine jobs.

UNIT 16

Look It Up

This unit is about:

- getting information
- using a table of contents and index
- using a dictionary and thesaurus

Think About

When you don't know how to spell a word, what do you do? Besides word meanings, what information can you get from a dictionary?

Look It Up

Rose must write a letter to a firm which has billed her plumbing supply company for a dozen wrenches. The wrenches have not arrived and Rose wants to find out why.

Rose knows that if she uses the correct **tone** and form, her letter will have more **authority**. This may help her to get faster results. To get some ideas on how to write the letter, Rose opens her secretary's handbook. She looks at the Table of Contents which is in the front of the book. It lists the chapters of the book in order. It also tells the page on which the chapter begins. It looks like this:

TABLE OF CONTENTS

Chapter 1: Letters	Page 11
Chapter 2: Reports	Page 43
Chapter 3: Meetings	Page 68
Chapter 4: Punctuation	Page 104
Chapter 5: International Trade	Page 129

Rose looks through the first chapter and finds several model letters. There is also a lot of good advice on writing this type of letter.

Rose wants to address the letter directly to the person in charge of shipping the parts. Her boss said the person's title would be "supervisor of shipping." Rose thinks that one or more of the words in the title should be capitalized, but she isn't sure. She looks again at the table of contents but doesn't see what she wants. Next she turns to the back of the book to find the index. The index lists the subjects of the book in alphabetical order and gives their page numbers in the book. A sample index is shown below.

INDEX

Abbreviations	19
Addresses	14
Business Etiquette	154
Capitalization	121
Geographic Names	127
Titles of Persons	124
Data Processing	86
Bank Services	88
Retrieval	97

Rose finds the information that she needs on page 124. She completes the letter and takes it to Ms. Johnson for her signature. Her boss is **impressed** with the tone and form of the letter and praises Rose for her work. However, she thinks the word "incompetant" is misspelled and asks Rose to check it. She also asks Rose to find another word for "hurry" because she used it several times in the letter.

Rose finds the dictionary on her shelf of **reference books**. She opens it and uses the **guide words** at the top of each page to quickly find the word. She discovers that she spelled the word incorrectly and she makes the necessary change.

INCLUDED   **INCORPORATE**

in clud' ed, *adj.* enclosed, contained
in cog' ni to, *adj.* regarding a person's disguise
in com' pe tent, *adj.* inefficient, without knowledge, ability, or skill

---

When Rose looks up the word "hurry" in the dictionary, she doesn't find any **synonyms**, or words that are similar in meaning. So, she looks in the **thesaurus** for other words which have the same meaning. The thesaurus usually gives only synonyms. Here is what Rose finds in her thesaurus:

      hurry   1. n. quickness, haste, dispatch
                    2. v. run, rush, hasten, speed

She chooses the synonym "rush" and completes the letter. Then she puts the three reference books on the shelf next to her desk. She knows they will be useful again soon.

REVIEW

Choose the best answer. Circle it. Go back to the reading to check your answers. The first one is done for you.

1. All reference books give _____.
    a. word meanings
    b. synonyms
    ⓒ. information
    d. guide words

2. The table of contents lists _____.
    a. the meanings of words
    b. the subjects in alphabetical order
    c. the chapters in order
    d. the correct spelling of a word

3. An index of a book tells _____.
    a. synonyms of a word
    b. the chapters in order
    c. how to write a letter
    d. the subjects in alphabetical order

4. Rose needs to find another word that means appreciate. Where do you think she should look?
    a. in a thesaurus
    b. in an index
    c. in a secretary's handbook
    d. in a table of contents

5. Why do you think Ms. Johnson was impressed by Rose's letter?
    a. It did not have any mistakes.
    b. She had misspelled a word.
    c. The letter was well written.
    d. She wrote it quickly.

6. Another title for this unit could be _____.
    a. Look in the Index
    b. How to Write a Letter
    c. Using Reference Books
    d. Where to Keep a Dictionary

PRACTICE

A   Pick a synonym. Below is a sample page from a thesaurus. Use the information in the sample page to find one synonym for each of the words listed below. Write the synonyms on the blank lines. The first one is done for you.

THESAURUS: SAMPLE PAGE

offset, v. counterbalance, compensate
often, adv. frequently, regularly, repeatedly
ogre, n. monster, fiend, goblin
oil, n. petroleum, grease, fat
old, adj. aged, mature, elderly
omen, n. warning, sign
ominous, adj. sinister, threatening, unfavorable
omit, v. leave out, disregard, ignore
onerous, adj. difficult, weighty, burdensome
only, adj. alone, solitary, single
onslaught, n. assault, charge, attack
ooze, n. mud, slime, mire
opaque, adj. clouded, obscure
operation, n. process, function
opponent, n. enemy, rival, adversary
opportunity, n. occasion, chance, convenience
oppose, v. resist, thwart

1. opaque oil   **clouded grease**
2. onerous operation _____
3. old opponent   _____
4. oppose onslaught   _____
5. often omit   _____
6. ominous omen   _____

97

B. Choose the best reference book. Which book would you use to find the information below? In the spaces, write **S** for secretary's handbook, **D** for dictionary, or **T** for thesaurus. The first one is done for you.

        S—secretary's handbook
        D—dictionary
        T—thesaurus

__S__ 1. How to write a business report

____ 2. The meaning of *onerous*

____ 3. Another word for *damaged*

____ 4. The correct spelling of *exaggerated*

____ 5. How to run a business meeting

____ 6. A synonym for the word *impressed*

____ 7. How to address an envelope

____ 8. The correct use of a comma

____ 9. If the word *alter* is a noun or a verb

C. Dictionary definitions. Most people use the dictionary to check the spelling, meaning, and pronunciation of a word. Dictionaries also tell the part of speech of a word (such as noun, verb, or adjective) and where the word came from (word origin). Read the dictionary definition below. Then decide if the statements are true or false. The first one is done for you.

    boss (bôss) *n., pl.* **-es** [Dutch *baas*, a master, uncle] **1.** person with authority over employees **2.** person who controls a political organization —*v.* to give orders to someone

	True	False
1. The word *boss* can be used as a noun or verb.	√	
2. *Boss* came from the Dutch language.		
3. It has only one meaning.		
4. The plural form of boss is bossis.		

D. Find it in the dictionary. Use the dictionary definitions below to answer the questions. Write your answers on the blank lines. The first one is done for you.

DICTIONARY DEFINITIONS

career (ka rir') *n.* [French carrière, road] occupation or profession —*v.* to move at full speed

eraser (i ra' ser) *n.* [Latin erasus, to scratch out] a device to remove marks

lunch (lunch) *n.* [Spanish lonja, slice of ham] **1.** any light meal **2.** food prepared for a light meal —*v.* to eat lunch

pen (pen) *n.* [Latin penna, feather] **1.** quill or feather trimmed for writing with ink **2.** any device for writing with ink —*v.* to write

salary (sal'a re) *n.,* pl. **-ries** [Latin salarium, money for salt] fixed payment for services given

1. What is the origin of the word *career*?   <u>**French**</u>
2. What is the origin of the word *pen*?   _____
3. What is the plural form of *salary*?   _____
4. What is the meaning of the verb *career*?   _____
5. How many meanings does *lunch* have?   _____

E. Use the guide words. The guide words *firepower* and *fish* appear on one page of the dictionary. Use these guide words to decide if the words below would appear on that page of the dictionary. Check **Yes** or **No**. The first one is done for you.

<u>**FIREPOWER**</u>   <u>**FISH**</u>

	YES	NO
1. firm	√	
2. first aid		
3. fireplace		
4. fir		
5. fireproof		

UNIT 17

Getting the Facts

This unit is about:

- finding information in a catalog
- filling out an order form

Think About

Have you ever ordered something from a catalog?
What did you have to write on the order form?

Getting the Facts

If the office needs paper clips, machinery parts or other supplies, a **supplier's catalog** has ordering information. This catalog gives a **description**, the cost, and the ordering numbers of the company's products. It is always important to use an up-to-date catalog because prices and products change.

To find the page of the product that you want, look in the index. Look carefully for the exact product that you need. Often there are several choices of size, style, color, and price. Be sure that you choose the right one. Then fill out the order form **accurately** and completely. If you make a mistake or leave something out, your order may be delayed.

Part of Rose's job is to make sure the office does not run out of supplies. Yesterday she checked the supply room and discovered that the office was getting low on file folders. To order a new supply, Rose looked through an office supply catalog. First she looked in the index to find the page for folders. The index told her to look on page 136. This is what Rose found:

FILE FOLDERS
Acid free; rounded corners with 1/2" exposed tabs; light tan color. 100 folders per package.

Cat.#	Tab Size	Size	Unit Price
31 46 386	Full Cut	$9 1/2$" x $11 3/4$"	$19.40/pkg
31 46 387	Half Cut	$9 1/2$" x $11 3/4$"	19.40/pkg
31 46 388	Full Cut	$9 1/2$" x $14 3/4$"	24.45/pkg
31 46 389	Half Cut	$9 1/2$" x $14 3/4$"	24.45/pkg

Rose read the description of file folders and noticed that they came in different sizes. To make sure she ordered the right size, Rose went back to the supply room. She looked at the remaining package of file folders and found a description on the outside. It said: File folders, Full Cut, $9 1/2$" x $11 3/4$".

Next Rose took one of the order forms from the catalog. She filled in her name and the office address. Then she carefully wrote in her order. She included the catalog number and the number of packages of folders that she wanted. Under "**Unit Price**" she wrote the price of one package of folders. She multiplied this number by the number of packages in her order to get the total price. This is what the order form looked like:

ARROWSMITH ORDER FORM

Date 8/23/92

Mail Orders:
P.O. Box 3308
Yuma, AZ 92314

Toll-free Ordering/Product Information:
1-800-372-8739

Bill To Account No.

Rose Parnell, Office Manager
Name/Title

Lawson Plumbing Supply
Library/School/Company

27 State Street
Address

Memphis   TN   38137-5100
City   State   Zip Code

Ship to Account No.

Rose Parnell, Office Manager
Name/Title

Lawson Plumbing
Library/School/Company

27 State Street
Address

Memphis   TN   38137-5100
City   State   Zip Code

Catalog #	Quantity pkg, bx	Description	Unit Price	Total Price
31 46 386	4 pkg	file folders 9 1/2" x 11 3/4"	$19.40 pkg	$77.60

Before Rose put the order form in an envelope, she checked it over carefully. She made sure she had written the correct catalog number, and she checked her multiplication again.

"It's important to get the order right the first time," Rose says. "One time I put in the wrong catalog number, and the company had to call me. That wasted time."

REVIEW

Choose the best answer. Circle it. Go back to the reading to check your answers. The first one is done for you.

1. The purpose of a supplier's catalog is to give _____.
    a. product information
    b. word meanings
    c. an index
    d. synonyms

2. What information did the catalog give about file folders?
    a. the color
    b. the size
    c. the cost
    d. all of the above

3. The unit price of file folders is _____.
    a. the price of a package of folders
    b. the price of your order of folders
    c. the price of one folder
    d. the price of three packages of folders

4. Why is it important to use a new catalog?
    a. It is usually bigger.
    b. It doesn't have up-to-date information.
    c. It has today's prices.
    d. It is easier to read.

5. To get the total price of her order, Rose multiplied _____.
    a. 2 x $19.50
    b. the number of packages times the unit price
    c. 2 times the unit price
    c. 4 times $12.50

6. Another title for this unit could be _____.
    a. How to Order Supplies
    b. How to Sell Products
    c. How to Write a Catalog
    d. Using an Index

PRACTICE

A Complete the order. You need to order the items below for your office. Locate these items on the sample catalog page and fill in the order form on the next page. Then, find the total price for each item. Use your own name and address on the form. The first one is done for you.

Need to order: 3 boxes of plain window envelopes, $5^1/_8$" x $3^9/_{16}$"
10 boxes of plain window envelopes, $8^7/_8$" x $3^7/_8$"
5 rolls of $3/_8$" banding tape
10 rolls of 1" banding tape
2 packages of half cut file folders, $9^1/_2$" x $11^3/_4$"

Sample Catalog Page

POLYAR BANDING TAPE 4.3 mils thick; 60 yds.

Width	Cat.#	Unit Price
1/4"	227 771	$1.10/rl
3/8"	227 772	1.50/rl
1/2"	227 773	1.90/rl
1"	227 774	3.75/rl

FILE FOLDERS
Acid free; rounded corners with 1/2" exposed tabs; light tan color. 100 folders per package.

Cat.#	Tab Size	Size	Unit Price
31 46 386	Full Cut	$9^1/_2$" x $11^3/_4$"	$19.40/pkg
31 46 387	Half Cut	$9^1/_2$" x $11^3/_4$"	19.40/pkg
31 46 388	Full Cut	$9^1/_2$" x $14^3/_4$"	24.45/pkg
31 46 389	Half Cut	$9^1/_2$" x $14^3/_4$"	24.45/pkg

WINDOW ENVELOPES 500 envelopes per box.

Style	Size	Cat.#	Unit Price
Plain	$5^1/_8$" x $3^9/_{16}$"	445 7816	$12.50/bx
Imprinted	$5^1/_8$" x $3^9/_{16}$"	445 7817	27.90/bx
Plain	$8^7/_8$" x $3^7/_8$"	445 7818	14.70/bx
Imprinted	$8^7/_8$" x $3^7/_8$"	445 7819	30.10/bx

ARROWSMITH ORDER FORM

Date _____

Mail Orders:
P.O. Box 3308
Yuma, AZ 92314

Toll-free Ordering/Product Information:
1-800-372-8739

Bill To Account No.

_____
Name/Title

_____
Library/School/Company

_____
Address

_____
City   State   Zip Code

Ship to Account No.

_____
Name/Title

_____
Library/School/Company

_____
Address

_____
City   State   Zip Code

Catalog #	Quantity pkg, bx	Description	Unit Price	Total Price
445 7816	3	plain window envelopes 5 1/8 x 3 9/16	12.50	37.50

UNIT 18

Stressing the Limits

This unit is about:

- causes of stress
- symptoms of stress
- dealing with stress

Think About

What kinds of things upset you?
What do you do when you get upset?

Stressing the Limits

Stress costs American businesses over $150 billion a year in sick days, medical insurance, and accidents. An estimated 110 million people take medicine for stress each week.

Stress occurs when the body is strained physically or **emotionally**. There are many different causes of stress. Money problems, lack of sleep, and difficulties at work are common causes of stress.

Stress becomes a problem when there is too much of it for too long. It can result in heart disease, cancer, lower back pain, and many other illnesses. People who learn to control or cope with stress improve their chances of a healthy life.

People react to stress differently. Anne's back has been bothering her since she started her new job. She also has trouble sleeping. Anne feels that her supervisor, Ms. Jackson, has been giving her too much work to do.

Ms. Jackson has headaches every day. She feels **anxious** and angry because her department does not complete its work quickly enough. Her boss has been complaining about it. Ms. Jackson is especially worried about Anne, who often gets to work late and barely finishes her work. Ms. Jackson doesn't want to fire her, but she may have to.

Both Anne and Ms. Jackson are experiencing symptoms of stress. The headaches and back pains make it even harder to work well. Ms. Jackson realizes that she and Anne have to **confront** their problems and make some changes.

Last year Ms. Jackson had training in **stress management**. She learned that the first important step was to identify the cause of stress. She and Anne talked about their problems and decided that they both needed to make some changes. Ms. Jackson told Anne that she needed to get to work earlier so that she wouldn't feel **overwhelmed** by her work. Anne decided that she could change her morning routine to get an earlier bus. She could also break her habit of worrying alone. She decided she would talk to one of her friends or to Ms. Jackson when she had a problem. Ms. Jackson decided to have a meeting with everyone in the department. Together they could discuss ways to get the department's work done on time.

Stress management includes four important steps.

- First, identify the causes of stress.

- Next, try to change the situation that causes stress.

- If you can't change the situation, try the third step: change your response to stress.

- The fourth step in stress control is physical exercise. Physical activity energizes the body and gets the mind off daily problems.

Stress, in limited amounts, can help us to get things done. Too much stress, however, can cause physical and emotional problems. Stress management can help to reduce some of the pressures of daily life.

REVIEW

Choose the best answer. Circle it. Go back to the reading to check your answers. The first one is done for you.

1. Stress management is _____.
    a. straining the body
    b. a problem when there is too much
    (c.) a way to control or reduce stress
    d. a cause of stress

2. What was causing stress in Anne's life?
    a. She didn't have a job.
    b. She was having trouble doing her work.
    c. She didn't like Ms. Jackson.
    d. Her children were giving her trouble.

3. What was giving Ms. Jackson headaches?
    a. She wasn't doing her work.
    b. She didn't have enough work to do.
    c. Her husband was sick.
    d. Her department wasn't completing its work.

4. Anne and Ms. Jackson had different _____ of stress.
    a. types
    b. symptoms
    c. amounts
    d. uses

5. What else do you think Anne could do to reduce stress?
    a. She could complain to Ms. Jackson's boss.
    b. She could start to get more physical exercise.
    c. She could find someone else to do her work.
    d. She could ignore the problem.

6. Another title for this unit could be _____.
    a. Managing Stress
    b. Getting Exercise
    c. How to Get Rid of Headaches
    d. American Business

PRACTICE

A What causes stress in your life? Some of the common causes of stress are listed below. Put an **X** next to the items which do **not** cause stress in your life. Look at the remaining items in the list. Put them in order starting with #1 for the most serious cause of stress in your life. You may add other items to the list.

_____   Family

_____   School

_____   Money

_____   Co-workers

_____   Health problems

_____   Future

_____   Friends

_____   Appearance

_____   Noise

_____   Work/daily routines

_____   _____
          (other)

_____   _____
          (other)

B. Does it increase or decrease stress? Read each of the sentences below. Decide if the situation or activity will increase or decrease stress. Mark **I** if it increases stress and **D** if it decreases stress. Discuss your answers with your classmates or teacher. The first one is done for you.

$$I = increase$$
$$D = decrease$$

D 1. Mary talks to her boss when something is bothering her.

____ 2. Fred ignores his headaches and back pain and tries to work longer hours.

____ 3. Dave goes out for a long walk every night after dinner.

111

_____ 4. Paul decides to make a budget so that he can solve his money problems.

_____ 5. Doris puts the bills in a drawer and tries to forget about them.

_____ 6. John takes a vacation.

_____ 7. Anita gets angry when the other employees arrive late, but she doesn't say anything.

_____ 8. Mike moves his desk to a quieter location.

C. How do you manage stress in your life? Choose one of the causes of stress in your life. Using the four steps in stress management, describe how you could reduce the effects of stress.

1. Identify the cause

   _____

   _____

2. Change the situation

   _____

   _____

3. Change your response to it

   _____

   _____

4. Get physical exercise

   _____

   _____

UNIT 19

What Makes a Good Employee?

This unit is about:

- good work habits
- characteristics of a good employee

Think About

What do you think are some good work habits?
What kinds of things prevent people from getting their work done?

What Makes a Good Employee?

Employers hire people to do a job. They try to choose people who will do a good job and get along with the other people in the office. A person who wants to keep his or her job has to do the work the way the employer wants it done. In return, the employee should expect fair treatment from the employer.

The newspaper ads below show some of the qualities that employers look for when they choose employees. The ads first list the basic skills needed to do the job such as typing, filing, or handling the mail. Then they list the personal qualities needed, such as dependability.

Receptionist/Typist Good phone manners, accuracy and communication skills a must.	**Secretary** Seeking person with pleasant telephone personality. Dependability and accuracy essential.
Secretary Excellent typing skills are needed. Must be accurate. Must be able to set priorities and handle multiple tasks.	**Clerk/Typist** Reliable person to handle varied office routines. Accuracy and pleasant phone manners needed.

Employers expect a lot from their employees. They expect them to be **punctual**, to arrive on time. They expect employees to be productive, to do their work completely and accurately. Too much **socializing** and too many breaks slow down the work flow.

Joanne had excellent typing skills and she completed her work quickly and accurately. But she frequently interrupted others and often complained about the company, her supervisor, and the other workers. Soon other people in the office began to complain. Joanne was fired because her personality interfered with the productivity of the office.

Some employers say that these are the most common reasons for firing someone:

- **absenteeism**, or missing work frequently
- stealing
- poor skills
- low productivity
- poor work attitude

Employees in an office are a team with a common goal—producing quality work. A positive attitude and **cooperation** are necessary to meet the goal. People in an office spend many hours each week together. They must learn to get along with each other. Employers expect **maturity**, keeping control of one's emotions, and **tolerance** of each other's differences. An employee must be **ethical**, or honest and fair, in the way she or he treats other people.

Employers are seeking people who have both job skills and cooperative personalities. These people will work well as a team to accomplish the goals of the business.

REVIEW

Choose the best answer. Circle it. Go back to the reading to check your answers. The first one is done for you.

1. Look at the Want Ads in the reading. What quality is required in all four ads?
    a. communication skills
    b. good phone manners
    c. ability to set priorities
    ⓓ. accuracy

2. Joanne was fired because _____.
    a. she had excellent typing skills
    b. she was not cooperative
    c. she finished her work too slowly
    d. she had poor phone manners

3. The word punctual means _____.
    a. angry
    b. productive
    c. to be on time
    d. to leave early

4. A person might get fired for being _____.
    a. punctual
    b. tolerant
    c. frequently absent
    d. cooperative

5. Which of these employees is not acting ethically?
    a. Harold gets to work on time each day.
    b. Sue drinks a lot of coffee during the day.
    c. Ted says exactly what he thinks is right.
    d. Jane takes things home from the supply room.

6. Another title for this unit could be _____.
    a. The Importance of Being Punctual
    b. Human Characteristics
    c. The Qualities of a Good Office Worker
    d. Why Joanne Got Fired

PRACTICE

A What does it mean? Read each sentence. Figure out the meaning of the **boldfaced** word by the way it is used in the sentence. Use the other words in the sentence to help you guess. Write your definition on the blank line. The first one is done for you.

1. If you want to be sure the job gets done, pick someone **reliable** like Raymond.

    <u>does what he says he will do</u>

2. You are not a child anymore. You should act more **mature**.

    _____

3. Luisa added the numbers **accurately** and got the correct total.

    _____

4. Fernando is always **punctual**; he has not been late all year.

    _____

5. The billing department is **productive**; no one there wastes time.

    _____

6. He is not **tolerant** of different ideas. He thinks his ideas are the only good ideas.

    _____

7. The company lost a lot of money because of **absenteeism**. On most days at least ten people didn't come to work.

    _____

B. Which qualities are important? Job ads often use the words below to describe the workers they want to hire. Check the words that describe you. Put a check mark in the column "I AM." Next, check the qualities that you would look for in a boss. In the last column, check the qualities that you would look for in a friend.

QUALITIES EMPLOYERS LOOK FOR	I AM	BOSS SHOULD BE	FRIEND SHOULD BE
Reliable	_____	_____	_____
Punctual	_____	_____	_____
Cooperative	_____	_____	_____
Productive	_____	_____	_____
Mature	_____	_____	_____
Accurate	_____	_____	_____
Tolerant	_____	_____	_____
Efficient	_____	_____	_____
Ethical	_____	_____	_____

C. How would you choose? You are the employer. On your desk are 38 applications for just one position as a file clerk. As you read through them, you discover many well-qualified applicants. Over the years you have found that people who have one particular quality usually make good employees. Which quality did you choose? Why? Write your ideas on the blank lines.

_____
_____
_____
_____
_____
_____

UNIT 20

Starting Out Right

This unit is about:

- starting a new job

Think About

Think of a time when you had to do something new. How did you feel?
That kinds of problems might you have on the first day of a new job?
How could you help someone else who was new on the job?

Starting Out Right

Her first day on a new job arrived. Edna was prepared with her social security card, her lunch, and a neat, comfortable outfit. She wished she felt as confident as she looked. Would she be asked to do something she couldn't handle? Would people like her? Would she get there on time? These are normal anxieties, or worries, which most people have on the first day at a new job.

Mrs. Sanchez, the **personnel director**, greeted Edna at the reception desk. "We are so glad to have you with us," she said with a big smile. "You know, you were chosen from a large number of applicants. We know that you will do a good job here." Edna felt better right away.

"We have an **orientation** program for new employees," Mrs. Sanchez explained. "It will help you to understand how we do things in this office. I will take you around the office this morning and after lunch you can begin work at your desk."

First Mrs. Sanchez took Edna to the payroll department to fill out several forms. She completed several other **questionnaires** which asked about her previous jobs and health. Next Mrs. Sanchez gave Edna a booklet about the company's **personnel policies**. These policies are the rules for employees to follow. There are also rules for management to follow. These rules ensure that all employees are treated fairly.

"And this is a **procedures manual**. It explains how to do the work in your department," said Mrs. Sanchez. "You can keep it at your desk to refer to as you work."

Mrs. Sanchez then took Edna on a tour of the building. She pointed out the emergency exits, the cafeteria, and the rest rooms. She explained what Edna should do in case of an emergency, and she showed her where the first aid kit was stored.

Next she took Edna to the department where the company stored its files. She introduced Edna to Sarah Haywood, the department supervisor, and to the other employees there.

"Maria and Jane, why don't you take Edna down to the cafeteria for lunch. When you get back, you can show her where we keep things here," said Ms. Haywood.

"Oh great," Edna heard someone mutter. "A new person to train. I hope she doesn't slow us down too much."

Mrs. Sanchez took Edna aside and said, "Don't worry. You will learn quickly. I noticed how carefully you listened. Sometimes the others feel **threatened** by someone new. They may be worried that you will do better than they do or even take their jobs. Just follow directions and do your best; they will respect you for doing your share of the work."

Edna thanked Mrs. Sanchez, took a deep breath, and joined Maria and Jane as they walked to the lunch room. "You'll like it here," Jane said. "We work hard, but the people are nice. And the food is great!"

REVIEW

Choose the best answer. Circle it. Go back to the reading to check your answers. The first one is done for you.

1. The word confident means _____.
    a. believes in oneself
    b. well-dressed
    c. comfortable
    d. late

2. What is the purpose of an orientation program?
    a. to select the best applicant for a job
    b. to teach basic office skills
    c. to show new employees how the office works
    d. to teach employees how to manage stress

3. Which of these do you think you would find in a procedures manual?
    a. instructions on how to set up memos and letters
    b. the company's policy on sick days
    c. employee names and addresses
    d. employment applications

4. When someone made an unkind remark, Mrs. Sanchez talked to Edna about it. Why do you think she did this?
    a. She wanted to make Edna angry.
    b. She was angry with Edna.
    c. She wanted Edna to quit.
    d. She didn't want Edna to feel bad.

5. What would you do with a procedures manual?
    a. keep it at my desk
    b. keep it at home
    c. throw it away
    d. read it and then throw it away

6. Another title for this unit could be _____.
    a. The Procedures Manual
    b. Your First Day on the Job
    c. Making New Friends
    d. What to Wear on Your First Day

PRACTICE

A. What is the purpose? Explain the purpose of each of the items below. Write your ideas on the blank lines. The first one is done for you.

1. Procedures manual   __a book that tells how the company__

   __wants the job done__

2. Orientation program _____

   _____

3. Personnel policies _____

   _____

4. Questionnaire _____

   _____

B. Show the person around. You are asked to show a new employee around the building where you work. About fifteen other people work there too. Write the 5 most important things you want to show the new employee on the first day. An example is provided for you.

1. __The fire exits__
2. _____
3. _____
4. _____
5. _____
6. _____

C. Write a letter. A good friend is starting a new office job in another city. She is very nervous about the first day. Write a letter to help her handle that first day with confidence. Write your address and the date on the lines at the beginning of the letter.

(street) _____

(city/state) _____

(Date) _____

Dear _____,

_____

_____

_____

_____

_____

_____

_____

Your friend,

_____

ANSWER KEYS

On Your Own: Inside a Small Office UNIT 1

REVIEW

1. b
2. c
3. b
4. a
5. d
6. a

PRACTICE

A. Who are they?

accountant   auto body technician
manager   office worker   owner

Job Description	Job Title
Repairs body damage on cars and trucks.	auto body technician
Manages the whole business, makes all important decisions. Hires and fires employees.	manager
Deals with customers, keeps records, answers telephones, opens mail, files papers, keeps the office running smoothly.	office worker
Checks records of money received and paid out, does the payroll.	accountant
Owns the business. May also take part in business decisions.	owner

B. Predict the questions. *(More than one answer is possible. Check with your instructor or tutor.)*

> **Job Description**
> Take charge of organizing and running a small office. Successful applicant will have excellent office skills, pleasant personality, and ability to work independently. Computer experience helpful. Applicant should be flexible and willing to learn.

Interview questions:

1. Do you have any experience working in a small office?
2. Have you ever worked on a computer?
3. What skills would you like to learn?
4. Have you ever done any filing?
5. What would you like about working in a small office?

C. What are your strengths? *(More than one answer is possible. Check with your instructor or tutor.)*

Skills	Excellent	Fair	Poor
Filing		√	

Personal Qualities	Details
Friendly	I enjoy meeting people.

Teamwork: Inside a Large Office UNIT 2

REVIEW

1. b
2. c
3. a
4. b
5. b
6. c

PRACTICE

A. Who are they?

file clerk   machine operator   office manager
word processing operator   word processing supervisor

Job Description	Job Title
Files and retrieves documents.	**File clerk**
Operates duplicating machines. Makes copies of documents, letters, and reports.	machine operator
Operates word processing equipment. Produces letters, documents, and reports.	word processing operator
Supervises workers in the word processing center. Receives job requests and schedules work.	word processing supervisor
Is in charge of supervisors and office workers. Reports directly to the department head.	office manager

B. What is the difference? *(More than one answer is possible. Check with your instructor or tutor.)*

Working in a Large Office	Working in a Small Office
You can get help easily.	You get to do different things.
The company may have good benefits.	You will get to know the people you work with very well.
You may get the chance to move up in the company and to learn new skills.	You might be given a lot of responsibility.

C. Who's in charge here?

Marie Datcher is head of the customer claims department. Over 80 employees work in this department. The office support staff is a very important part of the department. The office manager, Ms. Sheila Kaminsky, is in charge of a staff of 29. The three supervisors report directly to her. Mr. Ted Carter, Vera's supervisor, is in charge of word processing. The records management supervisor is Ms. Tanh Nguyen. The supervisor of the duplicating center, Renaldo Garcia, worked his way up from an entry-level position. Together, the whole office staff works as a team to provide important services to the department.

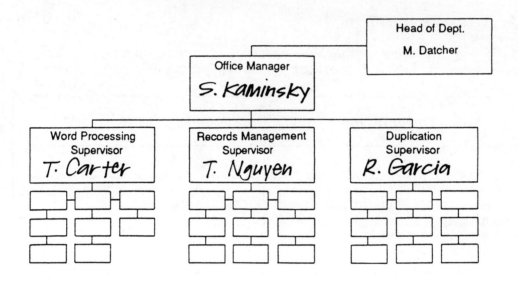

Following Through UNIT 3

REVIEW

1. b 3. b 5. c
2. d 4. a 6. a

PRACTICE

A. Put them in order.

_5_ The claims representative makes a decision.

_8_ Tony receives a letter.

_1_ Tony fills out a claim and sends it to the insurance company.

_6_ A word processing operator prepares a letter.

_7_ Copies of the letter and the claim are made.

_2_ The mailroom receives Tony's claim.

_4_ A file clerk retrieves Tony's file.

_3_ The people in the mailroom send Tony's claim to a claims representative.

B. Where is it done?

Mailroom   Claims   Accounting

Mailroom	1. Someone sorts the mail.
Accounting	2. Someone prepares checks.
Accounting	3. Payments from customers are received.
Claims	4. Word processors write letters to customers.
Claims	5. Someone decides on the amount of payment on claims.

C. Would you sign this letter?

RELIANCE INSURANCE CO.
"You Can Rely On Us"

January 12, 1991

Mr. Anthony Rivera
Ben's Body Ship
12 Main St.
Carbondale, IL 62901

Dear Mr. Rivera:

I am pleased to infrom you that your claim of 12/15/90 (Ref. # 679213) has been approved. The cost of the care provided by Quick Stop Clinic, Inc. of Carbondale is covered in full by your group health insurunce plan. Payment will be made directally to the provider. If I can be of further assistance, please do not hesitate to contact me.

Sincerely,

Sylvia M. DuBois

Sylvia M. DuBois
Claims Representative

---

    shop
    inform
    insurance
    directly

May I Help You?   UNIT 4

REVIEW

1. c   3. c   5. c
2. c   4. b   6. b

PRACTICE

A. Choose the best way to say it.

1. √   May I ask who's calling?
   ___   Who are you?

2. ___   What do you want?
   √   May I help you?

3. √   He's not in at the moment. May I take a message?
   ___   He's not here. I can't help you.

4. √   Good morning, Life Associates. Can you hold for a moment?
   ___   Good morning, I'm on another line. You'll have to wait.

5. ___   What are you doing here without an appointment?
   √   Would you like to make an appointment?

6. ___   What is your telephone number?
   √   May I have your number, please?

B. Make it polite. *(More than one answer is possible. Check with your instructor or tutor.)*

1. Why are you here?

    Do you have an appointment to see someone?

2. Why are you calling?

    May I ask why you are calling?

3. You can't talk to Ms. Ly now. She's busy.

    I'm sorry but Ms. Ly is busy right now. Can I take a message?

C. What would you do?

> **From the Desk of:**
> **Bruce Chen**
>
> To: Anna
> From: Bruce
> Re: Incoming Calls and Visitors
>
> 1. Put through any time
>   - Mr. Jason Burks (owner)
>   - Ms. An Ly
>   - Mr. David Berzinski
>   - all long distance callers
>
> 2. Take a message from
>   - Ms. Savan Phun
>   - Dr. Kevin Brown
>   - Mr. Julio Pena
>
> 3. <u>Never</u> allow in
>   - visitors without appointments

1. You receive a long distance call for Mr. Chen.

    I would put the call through right away.

2. Mr. David Berzinski asks to speak to Mr. Chen.

    I would put him through right away.

3. Dr. Kevin Brown asks to speak to Mr. Chen.

    I would ask to take a message.

4. A salesperson drops in without an appointment. He wants to see Mr. Chen.

    I would ask if he would like to make an appointment.

5. A salesperson calls from another state.

    I would put him through to Mr. Chen.

One Moment, Please UNIT 5

REVIEW

1. d 3. a 5. b
2. b 4. b 6. a

PRACTICE

A. Choose a word.

indicator lights   line   on hold   receiver   transferred

1. When Gerald's phone rang, one of the __indicator lights__ flashed on and off.

2. Gerald could not answer the caller's question so he __transferred__ the call to his supervisor.

3. Gerald put the caller __on hold__ so that he could transfer the call.

4. When the phone rang, Gerald picked up the __receiver__.

5. Gerald was talking on one __line__ when another person called.

B. What would you say? *(More than one answer is possible. Check with your instructor or tutor.)*

1. The caller wants to speak to Mr. Morgan, but he is not in the office.

   __I'm sorry, he's not in. May I take a message?__

2. You are giving a caller some information. While you are talking, a call comes in on another line.

   __Could you hold for a minute. I have to answer another line.__

3. You have asked a caller to wait while you take an incoming call. You now take the first caller off hold and start speaking.

   __Thank you for waiting.__

4. You have cut off a caller by mistake. The same person calls again.

   __Excuse me for cutting you off.__

C. Take a message. *(More than one answer is possible. Check with your instructor or tutor.)*

"Please tell Mr. Romero that Ms. Jane Miller of Duplex Services called. Yes, that's Duplex, D-U-P-L-E-X Services. It's not really urgent, it's about our appointment tomorrow. Tell him I simply won't be able to make it. I have to go out of town. Ask him to call me before 5:00 so we can schedule another meeting next week. Thanks so much.

To __*Mr. Romero*__
Date_____ Time_____

While You Were Out

M s Jane Miller
Of Duplex Services
Phone No _____

Telephoned		Please Call	√
Was in to see you		Will call again	

Message

She can't make the appointment tomorrow.
Please call before 5 p.m. to schedule another meeting.

By _____

Check the Time UNIT 6

REVIEW

1. c
2. a
3. b
4. c
5. a
6. a

PRACTICE

A. Time your call.

1. You want to call a friend in Oregon. It is now 5 p.m. in New York. What time is it in Oregon?

   <u>It is 2 p.m. in Oregon.</u>

2. You need to place a business call to a company in Ohio. It is 10 a.m. in New York. What time is it in Ohio?

   <u>It is 10 a.m. in Ohio.</u>

3. You promised to call your friend at 9 a.m. California time When should you make the call from New York?

   <u>You should call at noon in New York.</u>

4. You want to call a company in Colorado. The company opens at 9 a.m. It is now 11 a.m. in New York. Is it too early to call?

   <u>No. The company should just be opening.</u>

5. You want to call a friend in Texas. She usually goes to bed at 10 p.m. It is now 11:30 p.m. in New York. Is it too late to call her?

   <u>Yes. It is 10:30 in Texas.</u>

B. Choose a word.

conference call   international   participants   time zone

1. There were three __participants__ in the conference call.

2. Gerald made a call to England. It was an __international__ call.

3. Texas is in a different __time zone__ from New York.

4. Ms. Minh made a __conference call__ because she needed to talk to two people at the same time.

C. Choose the type of call.

conference call   local call
long distance call   international call

__long distance call__	1. Ms. Minh called someone in another state.
__local call__	2. Gerald called the bank in town.
__international call__	3. A customer in Mexico called Ms. Minh.
__conference call__	4. Ms. Minh talked to Paul Otaro and Jean Readon at the same time.
__long distance call__	5. Gerald called a customer in Nevada.

D. Arrange a conference call. *(More than one answer is possible. Check with your instructor or tutor.)*

Ms. Minh: I want to make a conference call to Paul Otaro and Jean Readon. Paul's number is (504) 554-3392. Jean's number is (304) 548-3301. Set the call up for 3 p.m. today.

_____

_____

_____

_____

The A, B, Cs of Filing UNIT 7

REVIEW

1. b
2. a
3. c
4. a
5. c
6. d

PRACTICE

A. Put them in alphabetical order.

Mountain Lakes Motel	<u>Anoka Cooperative Dairy</u>
Ben's Body Shop	<u>Ben's Body Shop</u>
Northeast Van Lines	<u>First State Bank</u>
Home & Garden Hardware	<u>Home & Garden Hardware</u>
Anoka Cooperative Dairy	<u>Mountain Lakes Motel</u>
First State Bank	<u>New Peking Restaurant</u>
New Peking Restaurant	<u>Northeast Van Lines</u>
Quick Stop Clinic	<u>Quick Stop Clinic</u>

B. What's your number? *(More than one answer is possible. Check with your instructor or tutor.)*

Number	Name
_____	_____
_____	_____
_____	_____
_____	_____
_____	_____

C. Going places.

Ames Business Supply
Los Angeles

Colonial Gift
San Diego

Choices Gallery
San Francisco

Taylor Rental Center
Bakersville

Wishbasket
San Jose

Serv-Tech
Fresno

Bakersville, Taylor Rental Center

Fresno, Serv-Tech

Los Angeles, Ames Business Supply

San Diego, Colonial Gift

San Francisco, Choices Gallery

San Jose, Wishbasket

D. What kind of system?

Example	Type of Filing System

1. OFFICE
   Meetings
   Memos
   Procedures
   Services
   Space
	Subject

2. 276-3002
   276-3306
   276-3812
   276-4183
   276-4529
	Numeric

3. PHILIPPINES
   Baguio
   Batangas
   Cebu
   Manila
   San Pablo
	Geographic

What's the Password? UNIT 8

REVIEW

1. c
2. a
3. b
4. c
5. c
6. a

PRACTICE

A. Label the files.

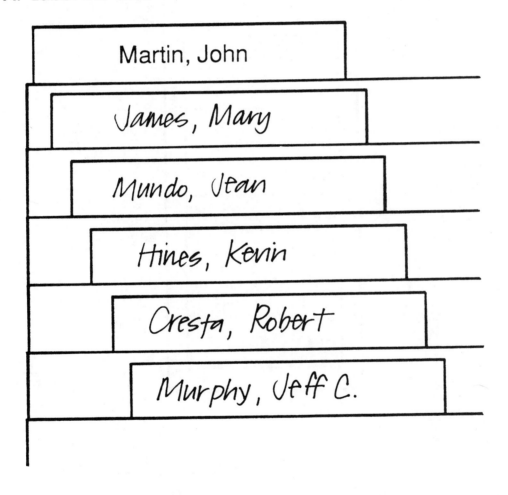

B. Which drawer are they in?

Ruen, Sam An
Zhang, Xia
Lyndon, James
Wallace, Ruth N.

Adams, David M.
Callas, Victoria E.
McGuire, Silvia J
Nguyen, Tanh Thi

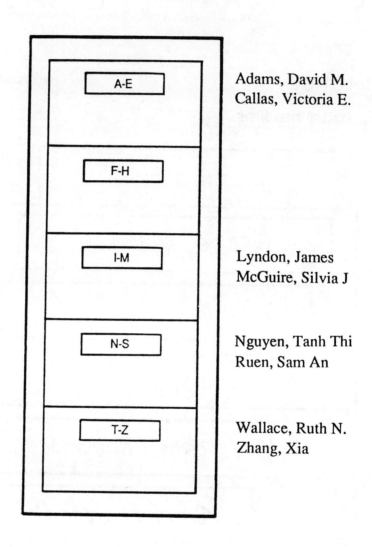

Adams, David M.
Callas, Victoria E.

Lyndon, James
McGuire, Silvia J

Nguyen, Tanh Thi
Ruen, Sam An

Wallace, Ruth N.
Zhang, Xia

Mail It UNIT 9

REVIEW

1. c
2. b
3. d
4. b
5. a
6. d

PRACTICE

A. What is the definition?

	A		B
_e_	1. insured mail	a.	a service that provides a record of delivery
_a_	2. certified mail	b.	put in order before mailing
_d_	3. deadline	c.	large mailings
_c_	4. bulk mail	d.	the time when something is due
_b_	5. presorted mail	e.	mail whose value is protected up to $400

B. Fill in the chart.

Class of Mail	Used for
First-class	mail that weighs 12 ounces or less
Priority	mail that weighs between 12 ounces and seventy pounds; mail that needs to arrive fast
Second-class	newspapers and magazines sent by companies
Third-class	large quantities of letters or packages
Fourth-class	packages of a certain size
Express	mail that must arrive quickly

C. How did they send it?

first-class   second-class   third-class   fourth-class
express   insured   certified

1. 200 presorted postcards telling about their business — **third-class** mail
2. the electricity bill — first-class
3. a letter asking for product information — first-class
4. a letter that must arrive the next day — express
5. a 20-pound package worth $100.00, no rush — fourth-class, insured
6. 100 bills to customers — third-class
7. a package with valuable drawings inside, no rush — fourth-class, insured
8. their son's birth certificate — certified

D. How do you want to send it?

	certified	insured
1. birth certificate	√	
2. wedding gift		√
3. passport	√	
4. tax payment	√	
5. birthday present		√

Preparing Outgoing Mail   UNIT 10

REVIEW

1. a   3. b   5. d
2. c   4. b   6. c

PRACTICE

A. Group the ZIP Codes.

02115 02291 02344 02131
02334 02256 02152 02380
02211 02112 02246 02377

021	**022**	**023**
02115	02211	02334
02112	02246	02344
02131	02256	02377
02152	02291	02380

B. What's the answer?

1. How does Dick send the 100-page report?

   He sends it express mail same day service.

2. Why does Dick presort the bulk mailing?

   He wanted to get the cheaper rate.

3. What does Dick use the telephone for?

   He uses the telephone to send faxes.

4. How does Dick decide to mail the package?

   He decides to send it fourth-class, insured.

5. What does Dick affix to the package?

   He affixes a mailing label to the package.

C. Fill out a packing list.

Sender: Ivan Clothing Co.
P.O. Box 52
Miami, FL 39402

Addressee: Linda Larson
1821 Mayfair Ave.
Costa Mesa, CA 98432

Contents:
1 girls' sweatshirt
2 pairs of boys' jeans
1 women's turtleneck sweater
1 pair men's gloves
1 pair women's gloves

Ivan Clothing Co.
P.O. Box 52
Miami, FL 39402

PACKING LIST
*Thank You For
Your Order*

SOLD TO
Linda Larson
1821 Mayfair Ave.
Costa Mesa, CA 98432

Quantity Shipped	Description
1	Girls' sweatshirt
2	boys' jeans
1	women's turtleneck sweater
1	pair men's gloves
1	pair women's gloves

D. Measure the parcels. Look at the measurements of the parcels below. Fill in the blanks with the length and girth. Then add the numbers together to find the total size. The first one is done for you.

1.
   length   __9"__

   girth   __30"__

   total size   __39"__

2.
   length   __12"__

   girth   __24"__

   total size   __36"__

3.
   length   __30"__

   girth   __44"__

   total size   __74"__

4.
   length   __30"__

   girth   __60"__

   total size   __90"__

From Words to Letters UNIT 11

REVIEW

1. b
2. c
3. a
4. b
5. a
6. c

PRACTICE

A. Using polite expressions. *(More than one answer is possible. Check with your instructor or tutor.)*

1. Send the package.

   <u>**Please send the package.**</u>

2. Where is your payment?

   <u>Could you please send your payment?</u>

3. Call Mr. Torres on Thursday.

   <u>Please call Mr. Torres on Thursday.</u>

4. You referred a client to us.

   <u>Thank you for referring a client to us.</u>

5. Send the check by Friday.

   <u>We would appreciate receiving your check by Friday.</u>

6. We want to see samples of your product.

   <u>We would like to see samples of your product.</u>

B. **What is the definition?**

	A		B
_e_	1. acknowledgement letter	a.	paper for business letters
_b_	2. purpose	b.	reason for doing something
_a_	3. letterhead stationery	c.	without extra words
_c_	4. concise	d.	communication by letters
_d_	5. correspondence	e.	written statement that something was received

C. **Be concise.** *(More than one answer is possible. Check with your instructor or tutor.)*

1. We were certainly pleased to receive your beautiful package.

   We were pleased to receive your package.

2. We here are looking forward very much to your visit soon next week.

   We look forward to you visit next week.

3. Here in this letter is enclosed a check for the services that you have provided.

   Enclosed is payment for your services.

4. We at Hansen Inc. are not at all pleased with the quality of the goods that your company has sent us by mail.

   We are not pleased with the quality of your company's goods.

5. Would you mind at all if we do not send the goods that you ordered until July 5th because Ms. Munoz is going to a wedding the day before.

   We will be sending your order on July 5th.

6. We heard that you are having some business problems so we would like you to send us a cash payment for our services immediately.

   We would appreciate receiving payment for our services immediately.

D. **Write a letter.** *(More than one answer is possible. Check with your instructor or tutor.)*

It's All in the Details   UNIT 12

REVIEW

1. b   3. b   5. c
2. b   4. b   6. c

PRACTICE

A. Find the errors.

1. Our office Christmas <u>patty</u> will be <u>one</u> December 15th.

   Our office Christmas party will be on December 15th.

2. We value <u>al</u> our customers' business.

   We value all our customers' business.

3. We look <u>fowrard</u> to hearing from <u>yu</u>.

   We look forward to hearing from you.

4. All <u>employes</u> must attend the <u>meetting</u> on Friday.

   All employees must attend the meeting on Friday.

5. This year, we <u>hvae</u> had a rise in sales in all departments.

   This year, we have had a rise in sales in all departments.

B. Correct the sentences.

1. The restroom is down the hall and to the right.
2. He is going to write a letter to his family.
3. We got in the car and drove to the office.
4. Where did you leave your umbrella?
5. It's important to use the dictionary to check the spelling of new words.
6. There are some letters in the mailbox.

7. This package is heavier than that one.

8. It's a good idea to take a break from proofreading when you're tired.

9. They took their coffee break at 3:00.

10. The letter fell out of the envelope.

C. Practice folding a letter. *(More than one answer is possible. Check with your instructor or tutor.)*

Getting the Message   UNIT 13

REVIEW

1. a   3. c   5. b

2. d   4. b   6. b

PRACTICE

A. Proofread the memo.

GREER WALLPAPER CO.
Interoffice Memorandum

TO: Jane Fox, Accounts Sup<u>ir</u>visor

FROM: Janine Muno<u>z,</u> President

DATE: September 1<u>5,</u> 1991

SUBJECT: Merrill <u>Acount</u>

Please remind the staff in your department that the Merrill account will be <u>revewed</u> on Frida<u>y.</u>

I will give a full report on the budget at that time.

mt

B. Proofread the addresses.

1. *Mr. Steven Spender*   Mr. Steven Spender
   32 Center Street   32 <u>Centr</u> Street
   Omaha, NE 68144-3155   Omaha, NE 68144-3155

2. *Farfel Design Co.*   Farfel Design <u>Col</u>
   10029 Buena Vista   10029 Buena Vista
   Los Angeles, CA 98221   Los Angeles, CA 98221

3. *General Manufacturing Co.*   General Manufacturing Co.
   5738 Western Drive   5738 Western Drive
   St. Paul, MN 55102   St. <u>Pal</u>, MN 55102

4. *Ms. Francin Jones* Ms. Francin Jones
   53 Pine Street 53 Pine Street
   Pontiac, MI 48055 Pontiac, MI <u>48054</u>

5. *Dr. George Franklin* Dr. George Franklin
   288 State Street 288 State Street
   Troy, NY 12210 Troy, <u>NU</u> 12210

C. Write a memorandum. *(More than one answer is possible. Check with your instructor or tutor.)*

<u>General Ideas</u>
you are having an office party for someone's birthday
you want people to be in your office at 2:30 on Friday
you want it to be a secret

Interoffice Memorandum

TO:

FROM:

DATE:

SUBJECT:

_____
_____
_____
_____
_____
_____
_____

The Electronic Office — UNIT 14

REVIEW

1. d
2. a
3. c
4. a
5. b
6. a

PRACTICE

A. Name the parts.

1. __printer__
2. __keyboard__
3. __screen__

B. Choose a word.

> delete   disk   entry-level   hard copy
> keyboard   screen   software   workstation

1. Marla makes a copy of her work on another __disk__.
2. You can read the information on the __screen__ before you print it out.
3. You can __delete__ words easily on a computer.
4. Marla uses a __keyboard__ to type in information.
5. A printer makes a __hard copy__ of your work.
6. Because he does not have much work experience, he is going to take an __entry-level__ position.
7. He spends most of the day at his own __workstation__.
8. __Software__ is a set of instructions for a computer.

C. Then and now. *(More than one answer is possible. Check with your instructor or tutor.)*

1. Twenty-five years ago an office worker needed to have good typing skills.

    An office worker today needs word processing skills.

2. The desks were arranged in rows, one behind the other.

    The desks may be arranged around the supervisor's desk or office.

3. All information was stored in filing cabinets.

    Information may be stored in computers.

4. Office workers carried messages from one part of the office to another.

    Office workers send messages by compter, intercom, telephone, or interoffice mail.

D. What's your opinion? *(More than one answer is possible. Check with your instructor or tutor.)*

   Companies can provide books and magazines that give information on changes in office technology.

In Good Time UNIT 15

REVIEW

1. d   3. c   5. b
2. b   4. a   6. b

PRACTICE

A. How does John spend his working day?

John works from 9:00 in the morning until 5:00 in the afternoon. He takes __45__ minutes for lunch, and he has a 15-minute break in the late morning. He spends __seven__ hours a day at his workstation. He always uses time during the day to __plan__ his time and organize his work. In the morning, he does the __urgent__ jobs first. This usually takes about __two__ hours. Then, for the rest of the day, he works on __routine__ tasks such as filing, opening mail, and writing reports that are not marked "urgent."

B. How much time does it take? *(More than one answer is possible. Check with your instructor or tutor.)*

How long does it take you to...?

1. cook a simple meal: _____
2. write a letter: _____
3. get dressed: _____
4. make a sandwich: _____
5. pay a bill: _____
6. take a bath: _____
7. eat lunch: _____

C. Put them in order.

__5__ Clear desk or work station. Put away supplies.

__2__ List the major tasks of the day.

__1__ Arrive at work on time or a few minutes early.

__3__ Do the jobs marked "urgent" or "important."

__7__ Go home.

__6__ Make sure all electrical equipment is off.

__4__ Do the routine jobs.

Look It Up UNIT 16

REVIEW

1. c
2. c
3. d
4. a
5. c
6. c

PRACTICE

A. Pick a synonym. *(More than one answer is possible. Check with your instructor or tutor.)*

THESAURUS: SAMPLE PAGE

offset, v. counterbalance, compensate
often, adv. frequently, regularly, repeatedly
ogre, n. monster, fiend, goblin
oil, n. petroleum, grease, fat
old, adj. aged, mature, elderly
omen, n. warning, sign
ominous, adj. sinister, threatening, unfavorable
omit, v. leave out, disregard, ignore
onerous, adj. difficult, weighty, burdensome
only, adj. alone, solitary, single
onslaught, n. assault, charge, attack
ooze, n. mud, slime, mire
opaque, adj. clouded, obscure
operation, n. process, function
opponent, n. enemy, rival, adversary
opportunity, n. occasion, chance, convenience
oppose, v. resist, thwart

1. opaque oil — **clouded grease**
2. onerous operation — difficult process
3. old opponent — aged enemy
4. oppose onslaught — resist assault
5. often omit — frequently leave out
6. ominous omen — sinister warning

157

B. Choose the best reference book.

S—secretary's handbook
D—dictionary
T—thesaurus

S 1. How to write a business report
D 2. The meaning of *onerous*
T 3. Another word for *damaged*
D 4. The correct spelling of *exaggerated*
S 5. How to run a business meeting
T 6. A synonym for the word *impressed*
S 7. How to address an envelope
S 8. The correct use of a comma
D 9. If the word *alter* is a noun or a verb

C. Dictionary definitions.

boss (bôss) *n., pl.* **-es** [Dutch baas, a master, uncle] **1.** person with authority over employees **2.** person who controls a political organization —*v.* to give orders to someone

	True	False
1. The word *boss* can be used as a noun or verb.	√	
2. *Boss* came from the Dutch language.	√	
3. It has only one meaning.		√
4. The plural form of boss is bossis.		√

D. Find it in the dictionary.

DICTIONARY DEFINITIONS

career (ka rir') *n.* [French carrière, road] occupation or profession —*v.* to move at full speed
eraser (i ra' ser) *n.* [Latin erasus, to scratch out] a device to remove marks
lunch (lunch) *n.* [Spanish lonja, slice of ham] **1.** any light meal **2.** food prepared for a light meal —*v.* to eat lunch
pen (pen) *n.* [Latin penna, feather] **1.** quill or feather trimmed for writing with ink **2.** any device for writing with ink —*v.* to write
salary (sal'a re) *n., pl.* **-ries** [Latin salarium, money for salt] fixed payment for services given

1. What is the origin of the word *career*?   **French**
2. What is the origin of the word *pen*?   Latin
3. What is the plural form of *salary*?   salaries
4. What is the meaning of the verb *career*?   to move at full speed
5. How many meanings does *lunch* have?   two

E. Use the guide words.

FIREPOWER **FISH**		
	YES	NO
1. firm	√	
2. first aid	√	
3. fireplace		√
4. fir		√
5. fireproof	√	

Getting the Facts UNIT 17

REVIEW

1. a   3. a   5. b
2. d   4. c   6. a

PRACTICE

A. Complete the order. *(More than one answer is possible. Check with your instructor or tutor.)*

Need to order:
    3 boxes of plain window envelopes, 5$\frac{1}{8}$" x 3$\frac{9}{16}$"
    10 boxes of plain window envelopes, 8$\frac{7}{8}$" x 3$\frac{7}{8}$"
    5 rolls of $\frac{3}{8}$" banding tape
    10 rolls of 1" banding tape
    2 packages of half cut file folders, 9$\frac{1}{2}$" x 11$\frac{3}{4}$"

Sample Catalog Page

POLYAR BANDING TAPE 4.3 mils thick; 60 yds.

Width	Cat.#	Unit Price
1/4"	227 771	$1.10/rl
3/8"	227 772	1.50/rl
1/2"	227 773	1.90/rl
1"	227 774	3.75/rl

FILE FOLDERS
Acid free; rounded corners with 1/2" exposed tabs; light tan color. 100 folders per package.

Cat.#	Tab Size	Size	Unit Price
31 46 386	Full Cut	9$\frac{1}{2}$" x 11$\frac{3}{4}$"	$19.40/pkg
31 46 387	Half Cut	9$\frac{1}{2}$" x 11$\frac{3}{4}$"	19.40/pkg
31 46 388	Full Cut	9$\frac{1}{2}$" x 14$\frac{3}{4}$"	24.45/pkg
31 46 389	Half Cut	9$\frac{1}{2}$" x 14$\frac{3}{4}$"	24.45/pkg

WINDOW ENVELOPES 500 envelopes per box.

Style	Size	Cat.#	Unit Price
Plain	5$\frac{1}{8}$" x 3$\frac{9}{16}$"	445 7816	$12.50/bx
Imprinted	5$\frac{1}{8}$" x 3$\frac{9}{16}$"	445 7817	27.90/bx
Plain	8$\frac{7}{8}$" x 3$\frac{7}{8}$"	445 7818	14.70/bx
Imprinted	8$\frac{7}{8}$" x 3$\frac{7}{8}$"	445 7819	30.10/bx

ARROWSMITH ORDER FORM

Date _____

Mail Orders:
P.O. Box 3308
Yuma, AZ 92314

Toll-free Ordering/Product Information:
1-800-372-8739

Bill To Account No.

_____
Name/Title

_____
Library/School/Company

_____
Address

_____
City   State   Zip Code

Ship to Account No.

_____
Name/Title

_____
Library/School/Company

_____
Address

_____
City   State   Zip Code

Catalog #	Quantity pkg, bx	Description	Unit Price	Total Price
445 7816	**3**	**plain window envelopes 5 1/8 x 3 9/16**	**12.50**	**37.50**
445 7818	10	plain window envelopes 8 7/8" x 3 7/8"	14.70	147.00
227 772	5	3/8" banding tape	1.50	7.50
227 774	10	1" banding tape	3.75	37.75
31 46 387	2	file folders, 9 1/2" x 11 3/4"	19.40	38.80

Stressing the Limits UNIT 18

REVIEW

1. c   3. d   5. b

2. b   4. b   6. a

PRACTICE

A. What causes stress in your life? *(More than one answer is possible. Check with your instructor or tutor.)*

_____ Family
_____ School
_____ Money
_____ Co-workers
_____ Health problems
_____ Future
_____ Friends
_____ Appearance
_____ Noise
_____ Work/daily routines
_____ _____
          (other)
_____ _____
          (other)

B. Does it increase or decrease stress?

I = increase
D = decrease

__D__ 1. Mary talks to her boss when something is bothering her.

__I__ 2. Fred ignores his headaches and back pain and tries to work longer hours.

__D__ 3. Dave goes out for a long walk every night after dinner.

__D__ 4. Paul decides to make a budget so that he can solve his money problems.

__I__ 5. Doris puts the bills in a drawer and tries to forget about them.

__D__ 6. John takes a vacation.

__I__ 7. Anita gets angry when the other employees arrive late, but she doesn't say anything.

__D__ 8. Mike moves his desk to a quieter location.

C. How do you manage stress in your life? *(More than one answer is possible. Check with your instructor or tutor.)*

1. Identify the cause

   _____

   _____

2. Change the situation

   _____

   _____

3. Change your response to it

   _____

   _____

4. Get physical exercise

   _____

   _____

What Makes a Good Employee UNIT 19

REVIEW

1. d
2. b
3. c
4. c
5. d
6. c

PRACTICE

A. What does it mean?

1. If you want to be sure the job gets done, pick someone **reliable** like Raymond.

   does what he says he will do

2. You are not a child anymore. You should act more **mature**.

   acting like a adult; grown up

3. Luisa added the numbers **accurately** and got the correct total.

   correctly

4. Fernando is always **punctual**; he has not been late all year.

   on time; not late

5. The billing department is **productive**; no one there wastes time.

   producing a lot

6. He is not **tolerant** of different ideas. He thinks his ideas are the only good ideas.

   accepting of different ideas even if you don't agree with them

7. The company lost a lot of money because of **absenteeism**. On most days at least ten people didn't come to work.

   frequent absences

B. Which qualities are important? *(More than one answer is possible. Check with your instructor or tutor.)*

QUALITIES EMPLOYERS LOOK FOR	I AM	BOSS SHOULD BE	FRIEND SHOULD BE
Reliable	_____	_____	_____
Punctual	_____	_____	_____
Cooperative	_____	_____	_____
Productive	_____	_____	_____
Mature	_____	_____	_____
Accurate	_____	_____	_____
Tolerant	_____	_____	_____
Efficient	_____	_____	_____
Ethical	_____	_____	_____

C. How would you choose? *(More than one answer is possible. Check with your instructor or tutor.)*

_____
_____
_____
_____
_____
_____

Starting Out Right

UNIT **20**

REVIEW

1. a   3. a   5. a
2. c   4. d   6. b

PRACTICE

A. What is the purpose?

1. Procedures manual __a book that tells how the company wants the job done__

2. Orientation program __a program to show new employees around the office__

3. Personnel policies __the company's rules__

4. Questionnaire __a form that asks questions__

B. Show the person around. *(More than one answer is possible. Check with your instructor or tutor.)*

1. __The fire exits__
2. __the different departments in the office__
3. __the bathrooms__
4. __where supplies are stored__
5. __who the other people in the office are__
6. __the place where people go for breaks__

C. Write a letter. *(More than one answer is possible. Check with your instructor or tutor.)*

(street) _____

(city/state) _____

(Date) _____

Dear _____,

_____

_____

_____

_____

_____

_____

_____

Your friend,

_____

GLOSSARY

This glossary provides definitions of the more difficult words used in this book. The glossary is in alphabetical order. The definition of each word tells how the word is used in this book. In the definition, the words in italics are also defined in this glossary. The numbers in parentheses tell where the word is used for the first time.

Abbreviation A shortened form of a word or words. We see and use abbreviations every day. The abbreviation for road is Rd. (Book 1, Unit 7)

Absenteeism Not showing up for work on a regular basis. He was fired because of absenteeism; he missed twelve days of work last month. Employee absenteeism increases when workers feel they are not being treated fairly. (Book 3, Unit 19)

Access To get into; to be able to see and read. When you access a file from the central computer, it comes up on the computer *screen* so you can see and read it. (Book 3, Unit 8)

Account number The number a company gives to each customer to keep track of bills. If you pay your telephone bill by mail, always write your account number on the check. (Book 2, Unit 5)

Accountant A person who organizes and checks the accounts of a business. An account is a statement of how much money is received and paid out. Accountants also advise *managers* on how money should be used. (Book 3, Unit 1)

Accurate Correct; without mistakes. He *proofread* the letter to make sure it was accurate; he did not want to send a letter with mistakes in it. (Book 3, Unit 17)

Acknowledgement letter A letter explaining that you received something. When Tony received the supplies, he sent the company an acknowledgement letter. (Book 3, Unit 11)

Active In use or ready to be used. Active files are kept in a place where they can be found quickly and easily. Files that are no longer active are called inactive. (Book 3, Unit 8)

Address The street, city, state and *ZIP Code* where a person lives or works. My *address* is 56 Maple St., Toledo, Ohio 45394. (Book 1, Unit 6)

Addressee The person to whom you send a letter. The post office will *deliver* a letter to the addressee. (Book 1, Unit 9)

Adhere To stick to something. Before mailing the letter, make sure that the stamp adheres to the *envelope*. (Book 3, Unit 13)

Adult education Classes for adults who are not in a regular school program. There are many places where you can take adult education courses. (Book 1, Unit 13)

Advertisement A notice of something for sale or a job opening. There are advertisements on TV, in the newspaper, and in the yellow pages of the *telephone directory*. (Book 1, Unit 3)

Affix To attach. Karl affixed a *mailing label* to the package. (Book 3, Unit 10)

Alphabetical order In the order of the alphabet. The words in a dictionary are arranged in alphabetical order. (Book 1, Unit 1)

Ambulance A special type of van for carrying people who are sick or hurt. The ambulance took him to the hospital. (Book 1, Unit 2)

Amount A quantity. He has $5000 in the bank. That's a large amount of money. (Book 1, Unit 10)

Annoy To make a little angry; to cause a little trouble. I wish the dog would stop barking. His barking annoys everyone in the area. (Book 1, Unit 4)

Anxious Worried; troubled. It is not unusual to feel anxious on your first day of work. If you feel anxious, try to think about something pleasant. (Book 3, Unit 18)

Apologize To say one is sorry. Gerald apologized for spilling coffee on my sweater. I apologized to the caller for cutting her off. (Book 3, Unit 5)

Appearance The way that something or someone looks. He is concerned about his appearance. He wants to look good for the *interview*. (Book 3, Unit 12)

Applicant A person who applies for a job. There were many applicants for the job, but Rosa had the best *qualifications*. (Book 2, Unit 11)

Application for employment A form that you must fill out in order to get a job. Applications for employment usually ask for *information* about education and *experience*. (Book 2, Unit 11)

Appointment A meeting at a certain time and place. She made an appointment to see the doctor at 3 p.m. (Book 1, Unit 13)

Appreciate To be thankful. In the letter he wrote, "I would appreciate it if you would return my check." (Book 2, Unit 9)

Area code A special number that is given to each calling area. In the United States, an area code consists of three *digits* such as 202 or 813. To make a *long distance* call, you must *dial* the area code before the telephone number. (Book 2, Unit 2)

Association A group of people who come together for a special purpose. Her town has a neighborhood association. This group of people plans ways to improve the area. (Book 2, Unit 20)

Authority The ability or power to control; demanding respect. She wanted her letter to have authority; it had to sound important. (Book 3, Unit 16)

Automated Using machines instead of people to perform certain tasks. If a system is completely automated, machines do all of the work. People only have to give *instructions* to the machines. By the end of this century, many office systems will be completely automated. (Book 3, Unit 7)

Benefits Good things in addition to money. Employers offer benefits such as health *insurance* and training programs so that *employees* will want to stay with the company. It is very important to discuss benefits as well as salary when you ask about a job. (Book 3, Unit 2)

Better Business Bureau An organization that helps people who have problems doing business with *companies*. When the company didn't send his order, he called the Better Business Bureau for advice. (Book 2, Unit 8)

Bilingual Able to read two languages well. She grew up in Vietnam and has lived in the United States for 15 years. She is bilingual in Vietnamese and English. (Book 2, Unit 15)

Billing period The amount of time covered by a bill. For most telephone companies, the billing period is one month. The *charges* on each bill cover the calls made during that month. He made seven *long distance* calls during the last billing period. (Book 2, Unit 5)

Birth certificate An *important* paper which tells when and where a person was born. You have to show your birth certificate to get a *social security number*. (Book 1, Unit 14)

Body (of a letter) The main part of a letter containing the *message*. In the body of the letter, she thanked her sister for the gift. (Book 1, Unit 11)

Boss The person who is in charge of an office or company; the employer. Everyone in the office works for the boss. (Book 1, Unit 5)

Brief Short; to the point; without extra words. I don't have much time. Tell me what the problem is, but please be brief. (Book 1, Unit 5)

Budget A careful plan for spending money. To make a budget, you think of all the things you have to buy for a certain time period. In a good budget, the cost of the things you need to buy is less than your *income*. (Book 2, Unit 16)

Bulk business mail A large quantity of packages or letters that a company mails at the same time. When Lydia's company has over 200 pieces of mail, they send it by bulk business mail. (Book 3, Unit 9)

Business A place or activity that sells a product or service. A bookstore is one type of business. An *insurance company* is another type of business. (Book 1, Unit 3)

Busy Not free; doing many things. I'm sorry but I can't stop for coffee now. I'm very busy. (Book 1, Unit 4)

Buzz To make a noise like the sound "z". A telephone or *intercom* signal is often a buzz instead of a ring. Another way to ask someone to call you is to say, "Just give me a buzz." (Book 2, Unit 14)

Calendar A list showing the months and days of the year. She wrote the date of the party on the calendar. She checked the calendar to see if she had any *appointments*. (Book 1, Unit 13)

Cancelled check A check which is stamped by the bank to show that it has been cashed. Cancelled checks are a *record of payment*. They show that you paid for something. (Book 2, Unit 9)

Certified mail A way to send mail that gives the sender a receipt and a record of delivery. People use certified mail when they send important papers. Walter sent his passport by certified mail. (Book 3, Unit 9)

Change-of-address card A card that people use to tell the post office of their new *address*. Before they moved, they filled out a change-of-address card. You can get a change-of-address card at the post office. (Book 1, Unit 8)

Charge The cost or price of something; an *amount* that the customer must pay. The charge for making a *long distance* call is higher during the day than at night. (Book 2, Unit 3)

Check A special piece of paper from a bank which you can use to pay for something. You must have money in the bank in order to write a check. If you have money in the bank, you can pay your bills by check. (Book 1, Unit 10)

Checking account A record of the money you have in the bank for writing *checks*. You must have a checking account in order to write checks. When you write a check, the money is taken out of your checking account. (Book 1, Unit 10)

Check-up A doctor's examination. It is a good idea to have a check-up even if you are in good health. Some serious problems can be prevented by regular check-ups. (Book 2, Unit 18)

Claim A *demand* for something. An *insurance* claim is a *customer's* request for payment of a bill. If you get sick, you must file an insurance claim. The company will study your claim and decide how much to pay. (Book 3, Unit 3)

Claims representative A person who makes decisions on *insurance claims*. A medical claims representative decides whether an illness is covered by the insurance plan. She decides exactly how much the company will pay for the care. (Book 3, Unit 3)

Classified advertising In a newspaper or magazine, a list of announcements about jobs, services, or things to sell. The announcements, or ads, are listed according to type. For example, ads that sell cars are together under a special heading. The want ads are part of the classified advertising section. (Book 2, Unit 12)

Collect call One type of *operator-assisted long distance* call. With this type of call, the person who answers the telephone at the other end must agree to pay the *charges*. (Book 2, Unit 3)

Combine To put or add together. When you make a cake, you have to combine sugar, flour, and eggs. When my husband and I pay taxes, we have to combine our *incomes*. (Book 3, Unit 10)

Command An instruction to a computer to do a specific *task*. The *keyboard* has special keys for giving commands to the computer. When you press the key, the computer will do a specific task. (Book 3, Unit 11)

Commitment A personal promise that you will do something. If you have a commitment to a job, you will do everything you can to finish it. (Book 2, Unit 19)

Communication Talking or writing between people in order to give *information*. Communication can be in person or *long distance*. Long distance communication can happen by letter or telephone. (Book 2, Unit 19)

Community A group of people who live together; the area in which a group of people live. There are several schools in our community. (Book 1, Unit 3)

Community calendar A list of announcements that tell you what is going to happen in the community. Social events, such

173

as dances and meetings, are listed in a community calendar. (Book 2, Unit 12)

Community services Private organizations that help the people in a community, or local area. Health care clinics and counseling centers are examples of community services. Community service numbers are usually listed in a special section of your *telephone directory*. (Book 2, Unit 1)

Company A business or *firm*. He works for a company that sells *insurance*. Some companies are very small while others are quite large. (Book 1, Unit 5)

Complete Having all the needed parts. An *address* without a *ZIP Code* is not complete. You must write the complete address on the *envelope*. (Book 1, Unit 7)

Complimentary Close A word or group of words used to end a letter. "Yours truly" and "Sincerely yours" are examples of a complimentary close. The complimentary close goes before your *signature*. (Book 1, Unit 11)

Computerized Operated or done by computer. In a computerized system, computers do most of the work. (Book 3, Unit 8)

Computer terminal Part of a computer system which includes a *screen* and *keyboard*. There may be many terminals connected to one central computer. Terminals are used to put *information* into a computer or to take information out. An automatic bank teller machine is one kind of computer terminal. (Book 3, Unit 8)

Concise Brief; using no unnecessary words. Laura's letters are always very concise; she never includes unnecessary information. (Book 3, Unit 11)

Conference call A special type of telephone call in which several callers can talk to each other *long distance* at the same time. Conference calls have to be arranged in advance. I have to be in my office at 4 o'clock this afternoon for an important conference call. (Book 3, Unit 6)

Confident Sure that things will turn out well. After talking to the *counselor*, she was confident that she would be able to find child care for her daughter. (Book 2, Unit 5)

Confront To face an unpleasant situation; to deal with something. He did not want to confront his money problems. Instead, he tried to forget about them. She confronted the manager with the fact that he had lied to her. (Book 3, Unit 18)

Consumer A person who buys goods and services; a buyer.

The consumers were hurt when the price of gasoline went up. (Book 2, Unit 8)

Contents That which is inside a box or other object. A *packing list* describes the contents of a package; it tells what is inside the box. (Book 2, Unit 7)

Cooperation Working together for the same purpose. Cooperation on the job is very important in any company or organization. If there is no cooperation, it becomes difficult to get the work done. The departments within an office must cooperate; they must work together to get a job done. (Book 3, Unit 19)

Cope with Handle problems and difficulties well. It is not easy to cope with both a full time job and all the duties of being a parent. (Book 2, Unit 18)

Copier A machine that makes copies of papers. Mel used the copier to make a copy of the letter. (Book 3, Unit 10)

Correspondence secretary A secretary who is responsible for preparing documents. Correspondence secretaries must have good writing skills. They must also be able to *proofread* and *edit* documents. (Book 3, Unit 11)

Counselor A person who gives help or advice. An employment counselor gives people advice about how to get a job. Other counselors help people with their personal problems. A good counselor listens carefully and tries to understand each person's needs. (Book 2, Unit 13)

Courteous Polite; having good manners. It is important for office workers to be courteous when they speak to customers. (Book 2, Unit 20)

Covered Protected by *insurance*. If you are covered by a medical insurance plan, you do not have to pay all of the costs for medical care. Damages or injuries caused by a car accident may be covered by automobile insurance. When you buy or agree to any insurance plan, always be sure you understand exactly what is covered. (Book 3, Unit 3)

Coworker A person who works with you. She gets along very well with her coworkers. He works alone. He does not have any coworkers. (Book 3, Unit 15)

Credit A way of correcting a wrong charge; repayment in goods or services. If you call the wrong number, the operator can give you credit on your phone bill. When you return an item to a store, they may give you credit instead of cash. (Book 2, Unit 4)

Cursive Handwriting in which the letters in a word are connected. You should use cursive when you sign your name on a form. Cursive is more difficult to read than printing. (Book 1, Unit 12)

Cushion To protect from breaking. He put newspapers inside the box to cushion the glasses. Some people use popcorn to cushion the *contents* of a package. (Book 2, Unit 7)

Customer relations Getting along with customers. In many small businesses, office workers come into daily contact with customers. They should try to keep good customer relations. In larger businesses, there are often whole *departments* that deal only with customer relations. (Book 3, Unit 1)

Customer service agent A company *employee* who helps customers with certain kinds of problems. If you are not getting good service from that company, you should call the customer service agent. When he couldn't pay the bill, he called the customer service agent for advice. (Book 2, Unit 10)

Customer service representative A *customer service agent*; a *company employee* who helps customers get good service. If you have a question about your telephone bill, call the customer service representative. (Book 2, Unit 5)

Day-care providers People or organizations that take care of young children during the day. A day-care center and a mother who takes care of children in her home are both day-care providers. (Book 2, Unit 13)

Dead letter A letter that cannot be *delivered* or returned to the sender. A letter without *postage* and a *return address* is a dead letter. The post office cannot deliver dead letters. (Book 1, Unit 9)

Deadline The date on which something is due. The deadline for Sam's report is Friday; he must finish the report by that day. The deadline for job *applications* is Monday. You cannot send an application after Monday. (Book 3, Unit 9)

Deduct To take away an *amount* of money, usually from a paycheck. Most employers ask you if you wish to have taxes and *insurance* costs deducted from your weekly paycheck. (Book 2, Unit 16)

Delete To take out or remove. The sentence was too long so she deleted a few words. It is easy to delete words when you are using *word processing software*. (Book 3, Unit 14)

Deliver To take something (such as a letter) to a person or place. The Post Office *delivers* mail every day except Sunday. Some post office *employees* deliver the mail on foot; others use trucks. (Book 1, Unit 8)

Demand Give an order. Young children sometimes demand things instead of asking for them nicely. A caller or visitor to an office has no right to demand things of an office worker. (Book 3, Unit 4)

Department Division of a company that does a special type of job. A large business has several departments. For example, there may be a sales department, a *records management* department, an accounting department, and a *customer relations* department. (Book 3, Unit 2)

Departure The act of leaving. Departure time for the bus is 3 p.m. The weather delayed his departure; he couldn't leave until later in the day. (Book 2, Unit 14)

Dependable Able to be trusted; *reliable*. A dependable person is someone you can count on. She is dependable; her employer knows she will do the work. (Book 2, Unit 20)

Description A statement telling what something is like. His description of my office was perfect. He remembered exactly what it looked like. Most catalogs will give a written description of a *product*. They may also show a picture. (Book 3, Unit 17)

Destination The place to which something is sent. The *address* on an *envelope* gives the letter's destination. If you do not write the *complete* address, the letter will not get to its destination. (Book 1, Unit 6)

Dial To press the numbers to make a telephone call. To get the *operator*, dial "0." (Book 1, Unit 1)

Dial direct To make a *long distance* call without the help of an *operator*. It always costs less to dial direct. Today, you can dial direct almost anywhere in the world. (Book 2, Unit 2)

Dial tone A long, steady sound you hear when you first pick up a telephone. This means that the line is connected and ready to receive your call. (Book 2, Unit 2)

Digit Any of the numbers 0 to 9. The number 345 has three digits. The number 4233 has four digits. A ZIP Code has five or nine digits. (Book 1, Unit 7)

Directory Assistance The number to call when you need a telephone number. He couldn't find my telephone number in the directory so he called Directory Assistance. (Book 1, Unit 1)

Discontinue To stop; to end. If you do not pay your telephone bill, the company may discontinue your service. (Book 2, Unit 10)

Disk A round piece of plastic used to record *information* electronically. There are different sizes of disks. She keeps her letters and documents on a disk. When she wants to work on a document, she must put the disk into the computer. (Book 3, Unit 14)

Dispatcher A person in a transportation company who sends out the taxis, trucks, or buses. When you telephone for a taxi, you speak to the dispatcher. The dispatcher tells the taxi where to pick you up. (Book 1, Unit 6)

District A certain area defined by a company or government. She is a district *supervisor*; she supervises all of the stores in that area. (Book 2, Unit 19)

Document A paper that gives *information* or proof of something. When you buy a car, you get a document showing that you bought the car. A *birth certificate* is a document that tells when you were born. (Book 1, Unit 14)

Duplicate copy An *exact* copy of a *document* or other paper. Before he mailed the form, he made a duplicate copy. He mailed the form and put the duplicate copy in his *files*. (Book 1, Unit 12)

Edit To make changes in the *first draft* of a document. When she edited the letter, she took out all unnecessary words. She also changed some words so that the letter would sound better. (Book 3, Unit 11)

Emergency A dangerous situation that must be dealt with quickly. A fire is one type of emergency. You must act quickly when there is an emergency. (Book 1, Unit 2)

Emotionally Having very strong feelings. After crying all day, he was exhausted emotionally. (Book 3, Unit 18)

Employee A paid worker in a company; a person who works for someone else. The telephone *company* has hundreds of employees. (Book 1, Unit 1)

Enclose To put inside. He enclosed a *packing list* in the package. She enclosed a *check* in the *envelope*. (Book 2, Unit 9)

Enter To put *information* into a computer. On a personal computer, you use a *keyboard* to type in, or enter, information. (Book 3, Unit 8)

Enthusiastic Very interested in something. The new office assistant is enthusiastic about her job. (Book 2, Unit 20)

Entry-level The lowest or first level. An entry-level position is for people with little work *experience*. Your first job will probably be an entry-level position. Many companies like to hire people at the entry-level.

Then they can train them to do a job in a certain way. When the person has some experience, he or she will be promoted. (Book 3, Unit 14)

Envelope A special cover for mailing letters. He *addressed* the envelope and mailed it. Don't forget to put your *return address* on the envelope. (Book 1, Unit 9)

Equivalent Equal to. Two things that are equivalent are the same in value or amount. One can take the place of the other. Many office jobs require a high school diploma or the equivalent. (Book 2, Unit 11)

Estimate To make a guess about something. If you have done something before, it is easy to estimate how much time it will take you to do it the next time. He estimated that it would take him about an hour to copy the reports. (Book 3, Unit 15)

Ethical Honest or just; morally good; doing what is right. That company took his money but did not send him the *product*. That is not ethical. Sue's actions were not ethical; she lied on the job application form. Jeff was acting ethically when he told the customers the truth. (Book 3, Unit 19)

Exact Perfectly correct; complete. I don't know the exact *amount* of money that I have in the bank. I think I have about $100, but I don't know exactly. (Book 1, Unit 5)

Expensive Costing a lot of money. A car is more expensive than a bicycle. (Book 2, Unit 6)

Experience Everything a person has done. Many job skills are learned through experience. Most employers look at a person's experience and education when they hire a new worker. (Book 2, Unit 11)

Express mail A class of mail which gets your letters quickly to their *destination*. She sent the letter by express mail next day service. The letter arrived at its destination the next day. (Book 2, Unit 6)

Facsimile machine (fax) A machine that sends a copy of a paper by telephone. You need a telephone and a facsimile machine in order to send a fax. Jeff used the facsimile machine to send the report to New York. (Book 3, Unit 10)

File box A special box for storing *folders*. A file box is a good place for storing *documents*. A file box is much smaller than a *filing cabinet*. (Book 1, Unit 14)

File clerk Person who works with files. A file clerk checks the *information* that goes into the file, stores the file, and finds it whenever necessary. A file clerk must be very *organized*. (Book 3, Unit 2)

Filing cabinet A large box with drawers for storing papers. A tall filing cabinet may have three or four drawers. (Book 1, Unit 15)

Financial hardship Problems with money; lack of money. The electric company has a *payment plan* for people who have financial hardship. (Book 2, Unit 10)

Fired Told by an employer not to come back to work; dismissed from a job. After many warnings about being late to work, he finally got fired. (Book 2, Unit 19)

Fireproof Cannot be destroyed by fire. A material that is fireproof cannot burn. Fire fighters wear fireproof jackets so they will not get hurt by fire. (Book 3, Unit 8)

Firm A business or company. Her firm writes *advertisements* for other companies. (Book 1, Unit 8)

First-class mail A class of mail for materials weighing 12 ounces or less. Most letters and postcards go by first-class mail. (Book 2, Unit 6)

First draft The first rough written form of a document. It took her fifteen minutes to make a first draft of the letter. Then she had to *edit* it. Writing the first draft of a letter is the first step in the writing process. The letter must also be edited and *proofread* before it is ready to send out. (Book 3, Unit 11)

Flexible Willing to change when necessary. A flexible person can stop what she is doing whenever something more important comes up. An office worker in a small business usually has to be flexible. (Book 3, Unit 1)

Folder A folded piece of cardboard for holding *individual* pieces of paper. He keeps his *important* papers in a folder. (Book 1, Unit 14)

Forward To send ahead; to send a letter to a new *address*. The post office will forward your mail if you fill out a special card. (Book 1, Unit 8)

Fourth-class mail A class of mail for sending packages. Fourth-class mail is also called *parcel post*. (Book 2, Unit 6)

Fragile Easily broken or damaged. Glass is fragile; it breaks easily. Wood is not fragile. (Book 2, Unit 7)

Geographic According to place, such as a country, state, city or town. A geographic filing system uses place names to keep files in order. Sales *departments* often use geographic filing systems because they sell the company's *product* in certain areas. (Book 3, Unit 7)

Girth The distance around something at its biggest part. The girth of this package is 45 inches. (Book 3, Unit 10)

Goal Purpose or aim; something you want to accomplish or do. A goal may be something you hope to do today or over your whole lifetime. For example, finishing a task may be your goal for today. Getting a diploma or degree is a goal that takes much longer. (Book 3, Unit 7)

Government agencies Offices that are part of the federal, state, or local government. Your state employment service is a government agency. (Book 2, Unit 1)

Graduate To complete a program at a school. She graduated from high school in 1990. (Book 2, Unit 11)

Guide words Words at the top of a page that show the range of words in an *alphabetical* listing. There are guide words at the top of each page of the dictionary. If the guide words are COMPUTER and CONTINUE, these are the first and last words on that page. All of the words that come between the two guide words are listed on that page. (Book 3, Unit 16)

Hang up To end a conversation by putting the telephone down. She said "good-bye" and hung up the phone. She was so angry that she hung up on him. (Book 1, Unit 4)

Hard copy *Information* which is on a piece of paper. When you type words into a computer, you do not have a hard copy of the information. You must use a printer to get a hard copy. (Book 3, Unit 14)

Heading A word or words that identifies a group of things. She wrote "apple" under the heading "fruit." (Book 1, Unit 3)

Heart rate The number of times your heart beats each minute. The average heart rate for an adult is 70 beats per minute. Running will increase your heart rate. (Book 2, Unit 18)

Hotline A direct telephone line or number which is used to give help or *information*. Emergency hotlines are answered any time of day or night. People can use hotlines to get free advice or help with serious personal problems. (Book 2, Unit 4)

Image A picture in someone's mind; the way people think of someone or something. That company can improve its image by doing better business; people will think better of the company. (Book 3, Unit 12)

Immediately Right away. They need someone for that job immediately. If you can start working today, they will hire you. (Book 2, Unit 17)

181

Impatient Unable to wait calmly. An impatient person does not like to wait. After waiting several hours to see the doctor, Jerry became impatient. He didn't want to wait any longer. (Book 3, Unit 4)

Important Of great value. It is important to have the *emergency* numbers near your telephone. (Book 1, Unit 4)

Impress To fill someone with admiration. She was impressed by his work; she thought that he had done an excellent job. His letter impressed me. I admire his ability to write. (Book 3, Unit 16)

Impression The way you feel about someone or something. If you have a good impression of someone, you like that person. Always try to make a good impression. (Book 2, Unit 19)

IN basket A large tray for holding papers, usually kept on a desk. An IN basket is used to store papers and letters that need to be answered or taken care of. When papers are ready to be sent out, they are placed in an OUT basket. (Book 2, Unit 19)

Income The money a person receives regularly in payment for work. You must pay taxes on your income. When she changed jobs, her monthly income went up. (Book 2, Unit 16)

Independently Without help or direction from anyone else. Some people like to work independently. They like doing things by themselves. They do not need anyone to tell them what to do. (Book 3, Unit 1)

In detail Carefully, paying attention to each small thing. When you read a story or job announcement in detail, you pay careful attention to each word. (Book 2, Unit 15)

Index A list of words, names, or subjects in *alphabetical order*. A newspaper index tells you where you can find things such as sports, weather, and *classified ads*. (Book 2, Unit 12)

Indicator light A light that shows something. The indicator lights on a car show which way the car is going to turn. On an office telephone, each *line key* has an indicator light. The lights show which telephone lines are in use. (Book 3, Unit 5)

Individual One of something; single. You can buy soda in individual cans or in a package of six cans. (Book 1, Unit 8)

Informal Not formal; relaxed. It's an informal party. You can wear blue jeans. An informal letter does not have an *exact* style; you can write it in different ways. (Book 1, Unit 11)

Information Things that are important to know; facts. You can get a lot of information from a *telephone directory*. He got a lot of information about his town from the library. (Book 1, Unit 2)

In stock Having a supply of something for sale; in the store. He bought all of the *envelopes* in the store. Now the store doesn't have any envelopes in stock. (Book 1, Unit 5)

Instructions Advice on how to do something. He read the instructions carefully before he filled out the form. The instructions told him to print or type the form. (Book 1, Unit 12)

Insurance An agreement to pay your bills in case of accident or sickness. His insurance paid for all of his medical bills. (Book 1, Unit 14)

Insure To make safe; to protect against loss. When sending something valuable, Rudy pays a little extra to insure the package. (Book 3, Unit 9)

Intercom Short for intercommunication; a way of talking to someone in the same office building. Office telephones may have an intercom button. It allows people to talk over the phone without making a telephone call. (Book 2, Unit 14)

International Between different countries; from one country to another. A call from San Francisco to Mexico City is an international call. International calls are more expensive than calls within a country. (Book 3, Unit 6)

Interoffice Between offices within the same company. An interoffice memorandum (memo) is sent from one office to another. (Book 3, Unit 3)

Interoffice envelope A large *envelope* used to send letters and *memos* between *departments* of an office. She put the letter in an interoffice envelope and sent it to the records department. (Book 3, Unit 13)

Interrupt To break in on an action or stop doing something. Sometimes you must interrupt your work to pay attention to something that is more important. For example, typing or filing work is often interrupted by the telephone. (Book 3, Unit 4)

Interview A meeting in which one person asks another person questions; a meeting to decide if a person will be hired for a job. At the job interview, he asked me where I had worked before. He interviewed several people to get *information* about the history of the town. (Book 1, Unit 4)

Job announcement A sign or advertisement announcing that a job is open. A job announcement usually has the name of the job, the basic *qualifications*, and a telephone number or address.

183

Job announcements may be found in many places, but especially in newspapers and on bulletin boards. (Book 2, Unit 15)

Key A list that explains what letters or symbols mean. The key is usually located at the bottom of a bill or map. On a telephone bill, for example, the letter "N" may stand for "night direct dial." Always check the key to be sure. (Book 2, Unit 5)

Keyboard A device used to type information into a computer. The keyboard is attached to the computer by a wire. A keyboard contains all of the letters of the alphabet, numbers, and *punctuation* marks. It also has special *instruction* keys. (Book 3, Unit 14)

Letterhead stationery Writing paper with the name of a company printed on it. Angela always types business letters on letterhead stationery. When she writes a personal letter, she does not use letterhead stationery. (Book 3, Unit 11)

Limit The greatest amount or number allowed. One sandwich is my limit; I can't eat more than that. The telephone company puts a limit on the number of free *directory assistance* calls. (Book 2, Unit 3)

Line key On an office telephone, a key or button for each telephone line. Every line key has its own number. To use a line, press the line key before you pick up the telephone. As soon as you pick it up, the line key will light up. This means that the line is being used. (Book 3, Unit 5)

Lobby A hall or room that you enter from the front door of a large building. Just go in the front door and you will be in the lobby. Houses do not have lobbies, but office buildings and hotels usually do. (Book 1, Unit 6)

Location A place or position. Can you give the *exact* location of your house? This town is in a nice location. (Book 1, Unit 2)

Long distance A telephone call outside your local calling area. A call from New York to California is a long distance call. (Book 2, Unit 2)

Lower case Printed in its small form (a, b, c) rather than in its large or capital form (A, B, C). When you sign your name, the first letter is capitalized. The other letters are lower case. At the end of the *memo*, Anne wrote her initials in lower case letters. (Book 3, Unit 13)

Loyal True to ones friends, family, or country; faithful. He is a loyal person. Whatever happens, you can count on him to help. (Book 2, Unit 20)

Mailing label A piece of paper with the *address* of the sender and *addressee* which goes on the outside of a package. She filled out the mailing label and attached it to the outside of the box. (Book 2, Unit 7)

Mail-order business A *business* that sells things through the mail. He doesn't go to the store very often; he buys most things from a mail-order business. (Book 1, Unit 10)

Manager Person in charge. The manager of a small business is in control of its day-to-day business. Jack asked the manager for a day off. (Book 3, Unit 1)

Marital status *Information* saying whether you are married or not. Many forms ask for your marital status. You must say if you are married or not. (Book 1, Unit 12)

Maturity State of being fully grown; acting like an adult. People gain maturity as they get older, and especially when they become parents. (Book 3, Unit 19)

Memorandum (memo) A note from one person or department to another within the company. Dave wrote a memorandum to the *employees* in each *department* of the company. (Book 3, Unit 13)

Message A piece of information spoken or written to another person. Could you give John a message? Please tell him to call me. (Book 1, Unit 11)

Miscellaneous Mixed; things that do not fit into any other group. She spends about $5 each week on miscellaneous items such as snacks, gifts, and postcards. (Book 2, Unit 16)

Misleading Causing a person to form an incorrect idea. The car's appearance was misleading. It looked new, but it was really five years old. (Book 2, Unit 8)

Money order A special kind of *check* which you can buy at the post office. If you need to send money through the mail, you can buy a money order at the post office. The person who receives the money order can exchange it for cash at the post office. (Book 1, Unit 10)

Money-saving tips Ideas on ways to spend less money. Here is a money-saving tip that can save you money on a new car: Buy at the end of the model year. Here is a money-saving tip from your *long distance* telephone company: phone in the evening when the rates are cheaper. (Book 2, Unit 4)

Nervous Afraid; worried. Some people get nervous before a test. Others get nervous when they have to talk in front of many people. (Book 1, Unit 2)

Net income The *amount* of money you receive after *deductions*. She makes a total of $18,000 a year, but her net income is about $14,500. (Book 2, Unit 16)

Night shift A work period at night. My sister works from 11 p.m. until 7 a.m.; she works the night shift. The people on the day shift work from 7 a.m. until 3 p.m. (Book 1, Unit 13)

Non-profit agency An agency whose purpose is to help people or to offer a service rather than to make money. The Red Cross is a non-profit agency. (Book 2, Unit 1)

Normal What is usual or average. His normal work hours are from 9 a.m. until 5 p.m. That is when he usually works. (Book 1, Unit 13)

Numeric According to number. A numeric filing system is easiest to use for businesses that have large numbers of files. Nearly all hospitals use numeric filing systems. (Book 3, Unit 7)

On hold Waiting at the end of a telephone line. When you telephone a busy company, you may be put on hold until someone has time to take your call. It is polite to say "Please hold" or "May I put you on hold?" before putting a caller on hold. (Book 2, Unit 14)

Operator An *employee* of the telephone company who helps people to make telephone calls. The operator helps people to make special kinds of telephone calls. You can get the operator by *dialing* "0." (Book 1, Unit 2)

Operator-assisted With the help of the operator. She made an operator-assisted call because she could not *dial direct*. (Book 2, Unit 3)

Opinion The way that a person thinks or feels about something or someone. In Kate's opinion, people should read more. In other words, Kate thinks people should read more. What is your honest opinion of that business? What do you really think? (Book 3, Unit 12)

Option Choice. If you have several options, you can choose whichever one is best for you. Telephone companies offer several different options at different prices. She chose the least *expensive* option. (Book 2, Unit 13)

Organize To put in a good working system. She organized her papers by putting them in files. It is easier to find your *documents* when your papers are organized. (Book 1, Unit 15)

Orientation Becoming familiar with a new place or thing. The purpose of an orientation program is to show new *employees* how the office works. Most companies will include a tour of the office in the orientation program. (Book 3, Unit 20)

Original Something from which copies are made. You make copies from original letters or reports. The *supervisor* asked him to make two copies of the original report. (Book 2, Unit 11)

Outgoing Mail Letters and packages which an office is sending out; mail leaving an office. Someone takes the outgoing mail to the post office. (Book 2, Unit 6)

Overdue Late; unpaid for too long. He usually pays his rent on the first of the month. It is now the fifteenth of the month and he hasn't paid the rent yet. His rent is overdue. (Book 2, Unit 10)

Overwhelm To become too big to handle. Job stress, illness, and other personal problems can sometimes overwhelm people. If you are beginning to feel overwhelmed, the first thing to do is talk to someone who can help you. (Book 3, Unit 18)

Packing list A piece of paper with the *address* of the sender and *addressee* and a list of the *contents* of the package. The packing list goes inside the package. (Book 2, Unit 7)

Paperwork Work involving the use of forms, letters, files, and so on. Some secretaries spend most of their time handling paperwork. It is important to keep paperwork organized. (Book 3, Unit 7)

Paragraph A group of sentences that give *information* on one topic. Tracy's letter had five paragraphs. Each paragraph gave information on a different topic. (Book 3, Unit 12)

Parcel post A class of mail for sending packages. Parcel post is also called *fourth-class mail*. (Book 2, Unit 6)

Participant A person who takes part in an activity. There were ten participants in the race. In other words, ten people ran in the race. You must make a *conference call* when there are more than two participants in a telephone call. (Book 3, Unit 6)

Password A secret word that is used to open computer files. A password is like a key. If you don't know the password, the computer will not let you access the file. (Book 3, Unit 8)

Payment plan A special plan which allows you to pay for something over a period of time. His payment plan allows him to pay fifty dollars a month for the next six months. (Book 2, Unit 10)

Pay raise Increase in salary; more money for a job. After she had worked for the company for a year, she asked the *manager* for a pay raise. They gave her a pay raise because she was doing such good work. (Book 3, Unit 15)

Payroll List of *employees* that receive regular paychecks and how much they earn. At the end of a pay period, an office worker makes out the payroll. That is, she checks the list and the number or hours worked by each employee. Then she makes out the paychecks. The *accountant* often helps with the payroll. (Book 3, Unit 1)

Perishable Food that spoils or goes bad quickly. Fresh fruit is perishable. Canned fruit is not perishable. (Book 2, Unit 7)

Personality The way a person is or acts; a person's character. Friendliness, patience, and a good sense of humor are part of his personality. In some jobs, personality is just as important as job skills. (Book 2, Unit 20)

Personnel director Person in charge of hiring new *employees*, handling employee *paperwork*, and suggesting rules for the workplace. In a large company, there is a personnel department where all employee files are kept. (Book 3, Unit 20)

Personnel policies Rules for employees. Personnel policies may include dress requirements and rules for overtime pay. Large companies often have their personnel policies in the form of a book that is sent to all *departments*. (Book 3, Unit 20)

Person-to-person One type of *operator-assisted long distance* call. When you make a person-to-person call, you ask to speak to a certain person. You give that person's name to the operator. If the person is not at home, you do not pay for the call. (Book 2, Unit 3)

Photocopy machine A special machine which makes copies of written material. If you need two copies of a *document*, you can use a photocopy machine. (Book 1, Unit 12)

Physical exam Medical tests to check a person's health. When you get a physical exam, the doctor will check many things including your *heart rate*. (Book 2, Unit 18)

Pile A number of things placed on top of each other. He put all of the bills in a pile on his desk. There is a pile of magazines next to my chair. (Book 1, Unit 14)

Postage The cost for sending something through the mail. What is the postage for this letter? (Book 1, Unit 9)

Postscript A short note added to the end of a letter (after the *signature*). He forgot to put his phone number in the letter so he wrote it in a postscript. (Book 1, Unit 11)

Preferred Wanted more than others. If a *job announcement* mentions that *experience* is preferred, the employer will probably choose someone who has experience over someone who does not. (Book 2, Unit 15)

Presorted *Sorted* in advance. Before taking the mail to the post office, the mail clerk presorted it. You will pay less money if you presort third-class mail. (Book 3, Unit 9)

Priority mail A class of mail for packages that *weigh* between twelve ounces and seventy pounds. Priority mail is faster than *fourth-class* mail. You can also send a letter by priority mail. (Book 3, Unit 9)

Procedures manual A book that explains how employees should do the work in that office. The procedures manual may explain the office filing system and letter writing *style*. New *employees* spend a lot of time reading the procedures manual. (Book 3, Unit 20)

Process To put through the steps necessary to do something. The *insurance* company must process many *claims* each month. Many people get involved in processing an insurance claim. (Book 3, Unit 3)

Product Something which is made or grown, usually for sale. That company makes a very useful product—soap. (Book 1, Unit 3)

Professional Having the skills needed to do a job well. Yolanda is a professional secretary. She has all the skills to do the job well. (Book 3, Unit 12)

Promotion Movement up to a higher position. A promotion usually means that you also get a *pay raise*. She was so happy about her promotion that she decided to have a party. (Book 3, Unit 15)

Proof of purchase A sales *receipt*; a paper which shows that you bought an item. If you want to return something to a store, you must have proof of purchase. When you use a money order, you keep the receipt. The receipt is a proof of purchase. (Book 2, Unit 8)

Proofread To carefully look over a piece of writing to check for mistakes. Kim always proofreads a letter before putting it in the *envelope*. She does not want to send a letter with any mistakes in it. (Book 3, Unit 12)

Punctual On time. It is important to be punctual. Other people should not have to wait for you. The company insists that employees be punctual. Everyone must be at work by 9 a.m. (Book 3, Unit 19)

Punctuation The marks used to divide words into sentences. You must use a punctuation mark at the end of a sentence. A period and a question mark are examples of punctuation. (Book 3, Unit 12)

Qualifications The training, education, and skills that make a person able to do a job. When you apply for a job, make sure you write down all of your qualifications on the employment application. (Book 2, Unit 11)

Questionnaire A form that asks for *information* and *opinions*. Some companies send out questionnaires to customers to find out how they can improve their *product*. (Book 3, Unit 20)

Rate Cost or *charge* for a certain *amount* of time. *Long distance* telephone rates go down in the evening. The lowest rates are on Sunday. (Book 2, Unit 4)

Reasonable Sensible. A reasonable *amount* of time is not too long or too short. It is just about right. If the cost of something is reasonable, it is not too *expensive*. (Book 2, Unit 14)

Receipt A written statement that someone has received money. When you buy something at a store, the salesperson gives you a receipt. If you want to return something to a store, you will need the receipt. (Book 1, Unit 10)

Receiver The part of the telephone that you speak into and listen to. The receiver changes your voice into electronic signals. These signals are carried through the line to another receiver. The other receiver changes the signals back into sounds that a person can understand. When you finish a telephone call, you hang up the receiver. (Book 3, Unit 5)

Reception area The place in an office where visitors are greeted. The reception area is usually just inside the front door of an office. There is usually someone in the reception area who can help you. (Book 1, Unit 15)

Receptionist An office worker who greets visitors. The receptionist is usually the first person whom visitors meet. (Book 1, Unit 15)

Record of payment A piece of paper showing that you made a payment. A *money order receipt* is a record of payment. It shows that you paid for something. (Book 2, Unit 8)

Records management *Department* or section of an organization that takes care of storing *information*. File clerks are part of the records management department. More and more workers in records management are learning to use computers. (Book 3, Unit 2)

Reference The name of a person who can give *information* about you. Some *applications* ask for personal references. Some ask for work references. (Book 2, Unit 17)

Reference book A book that contains facts or rules. A dictionary is one type of reference book. You can always find reference books in your local library. People do not usually read reference books from beginning to end. They use reference books to find specific *information*. (Book 3, Unit 16)

Referral A suggestion to go to another place for help or *information*. A telephone referral service tells you where you should call for the information you need. The *counselor* gave me a referral to a day-care center with several openings. (Book 2, Unit 13)

Refund A repayment; a return of money. He asked the company for a refund; he wanted his money back. If you return the clothes to the store, they will give you a refund. (Book 2, Unit 9)

Reliable Able to be trusted; *dependable*. A person who takes care of children must be reliable. A person who is not reliable will have trouble keeping any kind of job. (Book 2, Unit 20)

Remind To tell or cause someone to remember something. I have a doctor's *appointment* tomorrow. Will you remind me in the morning? (Book 1, Unit 13)

Reservation To arrange in advance to have something. He made a reservation for two people at the restaurant. When he arrived, his table was ready. If you are going to go by plane, you should make a reservation. You do not need a reservation if you go by bus. (Book 2, Unit 14)

Retrieve To find and bring back. Betty retrieved the files from the *filing cabinet*. (Book 1, Unit 15)

Return address The *address* of the sender. The return address goes in the upper left-hand corner of an *envelope*. (Book 1, Unit 9)

Right That which is due to you by law. In this country, you have the right to say what you believe. (Book 2, Unit 8)

Salary stub A record of the money your employer pays you. The salary stub is usually attached to your paycheck. It says how much you have been paid and how much has been *deducted*. It is a good idea to keep all of your salary stubs. (Book 2, Unit 17)

Salutation A word or group of words at the start of a letter. "Dear Jeff" is an example of a salutation. The salutation goes before the *body* of a letter. (Book 1, Unit 11)

Schedule A plan describing when to do things or when things will happen. You can look at a bus schedule to find out when the bus leaves. You can get a bus schedule at the bus station. (Book 2, Unit 14)

Screen The part of a computer that shows your words. When you enter *information* into a personal computer, the words will appear on the screen. (Book 3, Unit 8)

Screen To find out who is calling and why. Some managers do not wish to speak to all callers. They may ask the receptionist to screen all incoming calls. (Book 3, Unit 4)

Secretarial Related to the work of a *secretary*. A secretarial school teaches the skills needed by secretaries. (Book 2, Unit 16)

Secretary An *employee* in an office who writes letters, answers the phone, makes appointments, etc. A secretary must have many skills. (Book 1, Unit 5)

Section Part of something larger. A newspaper usually has several sections. You can read about the latest basketball game in the sports section. (Book 2, Unit 12)

Secure Closed tightly. If the bottom of the box is not secure, the *contents* will fall out. (Book 2, Unit 7)

Separate Not together; *individual*. Their children have separate rooms; they do not sleep in the same room. He put his bills and letters in separate folders. (Book 1, Unit 3)

Signature A person's name in his or her own handwriting. He forgot to put his signature on the *check*. Without his signature, I couldn't cash the check. (Book 1, Unit 8)

Small print Type that is very small, usually at the bottom of an important paper. Very important *information* is sometimes written in small print. (Book 2, Unit 17)

Socialize To talk or chat with friends. The best time to socialize with your *coworkers* is during breaks and at lunchtime. Too much socializing can interfere with your work. (Book 3, Unit 19)

Social Security number A number which the government gives to *individuals*. The number is used on an account showing money you have paid into the system. You must have a Social Security number to work. Today most people get Social Security numbers when they are children. (Book 1, Unit 12)

Software A set of instructions that tell a computer how to do a job. A computer cannot operate without software. A word processing package is one type of software. (Book 3, Unit 14)

Sort To put things, such as letters, in a special order. He sorted his papers and put them in *folders*. She sorted her papers so she could find them easily. (Book 1, Unit 7)

Specialized Having specific jobs to do. In large offices, workers are usually more specialized than they are in a small office. They are trained to do one or two tasks very well. (Book 3, Unit 7)

Station-to-station A *long distance* call made by *dialing direct* or with the help of the *operator*. When you make a station-to-station call, you agree to speak to anyone who picks up the phone. (Book 2, Unit 3)

Stress Strain or pressure people sometimes feel because of problems at work or home. Many things in life cause stress. Office workers are under stress when there is a lot of work to do in a very short time. (Book 2, Unit 18)

Stress management. A plan for dealing with *stress*. Some people take courses in stress management. These courses teach you how to *cope with* stress. Stress management usually includes exercise, good eating habits, and relaxation. (Book 3, Unit 18)

Style The way in which something is done. Pat uses the same style for all her letters. When Jean changed jobs, she had to learn a new letter writing style. (Book 3, Unit 13)

Subject According to topics. Some offices file their documents according to subject. Examples of subjects in an office filing system are "meetings," "accounts payable," and "personnel." In order to find a letter or document, you must look under the right subject heading. (Book 3, Unit 7)

Suggestion An idea given to someone. His suggestions helped us to make a decision. (Book 1, Unit 5)

Supervisor The person in charge of an office or group of workers. A supervisor is responsible for seeing that work gets done on time. Part of a supervisor's job is also to help workers who have problems or questions. (Book 2, Unit 19)

Supplier's catalog A book that lists the things that you can buy from a company. She ordered a new office chair from a supplier's catalog. (Book 3, Unit 17)

Support staff The office workers and supervisors in any organization. The support staff make it possible for other company *employees* to do their jobs. No large business could operate without a good support staff. (Book 3, Unit 2)

Symptom A sign that something is wrong; something that hurts or is wrong when you are not well. A headache may be a symptom of a cold. (Book 2, Unit 18)

Synonym A word that is similar in meaning to another word. A synonym for "big" is "large." (Book 3, Unit 16)

Take down To write down; to record in writing. Let me take down your address so I won't forget it. (Book 1, Unit 4)

Task A piece of work. An office worker may have many tasks to do during the day. It is sometimes difficult to decide which task you should complete first. (Book 3, Unit 4)

Telephone directory A book listing the phone numbers of *individuals* and *businesses*. Each city has its own telephone directory. If you don't know someone's phone number, you can look it up in the telephone directory. (Book 1, Unit 1)

Thesaurus A book that gives *synonyms*. A thesaurus is helpful when you want to find different ways to say things. She could not think of a synonym for "expensive," so she looked it up in her thesaurus. (Book 3, Unit 16)

Threatened Placed in a position of danger. An office worker who feels that her job is threatened is afraid of getting fired. A threatened person is sure to feel *anxious*. (Book 3, Unit 20)

Time zone A large area that keeps the same time. California and Oregon are in the same time zone. When it is 8 a.m. in California, it is 8 a.m. in Oregon. There are 24 different time zones in the world. (Book 2, Unit 2)

Tolerance Ability to get along with people who have different opinions; the ability to accept other points of view. Sue does not have much tolerance for people who disagree with her. Workers in an office must be tolerant of each other's differences. (Book 3, Unit 19)

Toll-free Without any *charge*. All telephone numbers with the *area code* "800" are toll-free. Most of the highways in the United States are toll-free. (Book 2, Unit 4)

Tone A particular way of expressing something; a special quality of words. His letter had an angry tone. He did not say that he was angry, but the way he used the words made me think he was angry. (Book 3, Unit 16)

Trainee Person who is learning to do a job. A trainee usually gets paid less than other more *experienced* workers. She started as a trainee in records management. Now she is in charge of the whole *department*. (Book 3, Unit 2)

Transaction A piece of business; a business deal or agreement. He kept a *record* of all his transactions with that company. The bank keeps a record of all transactions. (Book 2, Unit 9)

Transfer To pass a telephone call to another person. When you transfer a telephone call, you send the call to another place. Each telephone system has its own way of transferring calls. To learn how to transfer a call, read the *instructions* or ask someone to show you. (Book 1, Unit 15)

Tuition The charge for a course. She had to save money to pay the tuition. Tuition has gone up recently; it now costs more to take a course. (Book 2, Unit 16)

Typewriter A machine used for writing letters, forms, etc. To fill out this form, you should use a typewriter. (Book 1, Unit 12)

Unit price The cost of one item. The unit price of that paper is $4.00 a box. In other words, each box costs $4.00. (Book 3, Unit 17)

Update To bring up to date or make the latest changes. To update your *application* is to add new *information* to it. If you change telephone numbers, it is a good idea to update your application. (Book 2, Unit 17)

Urgent Needing quick attention or action. Mail marked "URGENT" should be opened before any other letters or memos. An urgent task cannot be put off until another time. (Book 3, Unit 15)

Waiting list A list of names of people who are waiting for something. The names at the top of a waiting list are the people who have waited the longest. If an apartment building is full but your name is near the top of the waiting list, you have a good chance to get in when somebody leaves. (Book 2, Unit 13)

Weigh To find out how heavy something is. How much do you weigh? The post office will weigh your letter and tell you what the *postage* is. (Book 1, Unit 9)

White pages The pages in the *telephone directory* which list the names of people in *alphabetical order*. In small towns the white pages are in the front of the telephone directory. In large cities the white pages are in a separate book. (Book 1, Unit 1)

Word processing A system for quickly putting words and information into a form that you can read. Word processing is similar to typing, but it is faster. You use a special machine, or *word processor*, to do the work. (Book 3, Unit 2)

Word processor A person who can use a *word processing* machine to write letters, reports, and so on. Also the machine itself. Nowadays, most word processing is done on computers. A word processor must have basic typing and computer skills. (Book 2, Unit 15)

Workstation In an office, the place where each *employee* works at a personal computer or terminal. Each workstation may have a computer desk, shelves, and a good office chair. Workstations are often arranged around the *supervisor's* office. (Book 3, Unit 14)

ZIP Code Numbers which give the *location* of a place in the United States. The ZIP Code is the last part of an *address*. (Book 1, Unit 7)